# RETURN HOME

# HILDA CASTAÑEDA

# RETURN HOME

*From darkness to the light:
a story of transformation*

**Return Home**

*From darkness to the light: a story of transformation*

**KIPIT** DIGITAL
Ediciones

Mariana Alfaro
Art Direction

Karla García
Project Director

D. R. c 2025, Hilda Castañeda
First edition, January 2025

It is prohibited to copy, reproduce in part or in whole, distribute, or use this work in electronic or other existing formats without the editors' and author's prior written permission.

*To the only one who left the ninety-nine sheep to rescue me: Jesus.*

*To my mother, who never stopped praying for me,
and to my father, who is and will always be a great lesson in my life.
To my husband: thank you for always supporting me in everything.*

*To my sisters, brothers, nieces, and nephews:
you are everything to me.*

*What man of you, having a hundred sheep, if he loses one of them, does not leave the ninety-nine in the wilderness, and go after that which is lost until he finds it? And when he has found it, he puts it on his shoulders for joy; and when he comes Home, he calls together his friends and neighbors, saying to them, "Rejoice with me, for I have found my sheep that was lost. I tell you, there will be more joy in heaven over one sinner who repents than over ninety-nine righteous persons who do not need to repent."*

*Luke 15:4-7 (NKJV)*

*I owe it to God and to you to write these words. He has allowed me to express my story on these pages, and He has worked miraculously and beautifully in my life.*

*Have you ever doubted the purpose of your life? I invite you to join me on a journey of discovery, where I found something bigger than myself. I hope that when you reach the last page, you will realize and understand that God places you in special situations for a specific purpose.*

*Even when we don't recognize it at the moment, there are times when the Lord works in the midst of darkness, and His light is about to shine through. His light will always come. God will never reject you, even if your life has been filled with mistakes and sinful choices. On the contrary, He will heal you, restore you, and reward you for the years of struggle caused by disobedience. Right now, He is waiting for you to return Home. Don't disregard what you cannot yet understand. The conflicts and chaos in your life may be signs that a miracle is coming. Open the doors to allow a supernatural work to take place in your life.*

*Your life will never be the same again. Do not fear at any moment. Just trust in the process that God will lead you through because sometimes He uses our deepest pain as a launching pad for our greatest calling. Let Him work in you because He has a very great purpose for your life. He wants to take you out of darkness into His wonderful light.*

# Introduction

The lights on the streets, the decorations and the happy figures announce Christmas.

Everything shines, and despite the cold that spreads over the city, the Christmas season offers with its colors and sparkles a warmth that the world has cultivated for centuries to commemorate the birth of Jesus, although perhaps in many places, the true essence of this event has been lost, why we celebrate and for what.

I arrive at the Home of my loved ones to celebrate with my family; everyone is gathered in harmony and happiness. Everyone laughs in that Home full of decorations and joy, my nephews run happily around the house, my brothers and sisters chat animatedly, time passes quickly while the preparations for Christmas dinner advance, everyone is excited about the family gathering.

On the tree the gifts represent love and dreams, the atmosphere takes me back to my childhood and the way I celebrated Christmas with my parents. It excites me to remember my family in those days of Christmas excitement, although a few years ago, I felt that that excitement was no longer in my life. At some point, it had ended.

Suddenly, I return to my present and look at the Christmas decorations, the bright lights in the house, and the beautiful decor. But I am sad. I feel a great emptiness in my being, a desire to cry accompanied by a feeling of bitterness, orphanhood, and infinite nostalgia.

I feel a massive hole in my existence and make a great effort not to cry. I try to think of other things that will take me out of this sadness, but it is challenging to get rid of this sorrow. I know that I am a successful woman who is hard-working and very good at what I do; I am a businesswoman who has grown through effort, dedication, and discipline.

I have overcome many difficulties, and now I am a winner in the business world, but there is a vast emptiness in me, a feeling of desolation that saddens me. Maybe because I always wanted to have a child and I did not achieve it; perhaps because I dedicated many years of my life to material things, and today, I realize that I neglected the spiritual side, the presence of God in my days.

Maybe the effort to grow in the business world, to show in this context that I could face any challenge, destroyed my sensitive side, or perhaps I neglected the true purpose of life, and today I feel alone and sad, without finding a reason to live ...

Thank you for being with me in this confession, dear reader. My name is Hilda Castañeda, and I am very excited that you read my words because this woman who described herself is me. This confused and sad woman is who I was a few years ago; today, my life is totally different, full of faith and hope, with a well-defined purpose here where I am and with the certainty of knowing where I am going.

# INTRODUCTION

Before you continue reading these pages, I want to tell you that this book is for you, yes, for you if at any time you have doubted the purpose of your life, you have felt an enormous void in your existence, and you are looking for something supernatural that will transform your life.

Through these pages, you will discover who Hilda is, who is that woman who had no meaning or purpose in life, who was running away from a truth that she already knew and from which she had moved away, causing a lack of identity and a huge void, to feel confused and unhappy, severely depressed and dissatisfied with her life regardless of her achievements or how many successes or material things she obtained, with childhood traumas and hidden pains even though she had searched for many answers and had tried everything without anything working for her.

You will know of my confusion, my impatience, and my overwhelming loneliness until the day when a supernatural miracle, a new opportunity, appeared in my life to transform it completely.

From that prodigious event came the "great purpose of life" so sought after by the world and so challenging to find. Still, it finally appeared before me without being clear about how it would arrive, without knowing how or under what circumstances it would be.

God's word is very clear about our life's purpose. Men in both the Old and New Testaments searched for and discovered that purpose.

Solomon, the wisest man who ever lived, discovered the emptiness of existence when one lives only for this world. Solomon reveals to us: "The end of all we have heard is this: Fear God and keep His commandments, for this is the whole purpose of a man. For God will bring every work into judgment, with every secret thing, whether good or evil" (Ecclesiastes 12:13-14).

Solomon says that the whole purpose of life is to honor God with our thoughts and lives, keeping His commandments, because one day we will stand before Him in judgment. Part of our purpose in life is to fear God and obey Him.

**No matter how old you are or what you have done or have not done, it is never too late for you to recognize the place where you belong. And if you are going through many struggles in your life, it is because God is calling you to return Home. This will cause your life to completely turn around, and you will find the answers to all those stumbles you have had: it will save your life. Return Home.**

I must confess something to you: if you receive a great blessing, something supernatural and extraordinary at some point in your life, you should not keep it to yourself. It would be best if you shouted it from the rooftops. I will tell you why I think so. I did not see the great blessing that came into my life to become a great transformation coming.

The process has not been easy because my human mind could not understand how to escape that life of disasters, confusion, and chaos. Still, I managed it (I did not do it alone with my strength but thanks to a supernatural power).

Now, I have a life of great hope because I know that there is something much greater than the riches of this world that awaits me, something divine and marvelous where I can see streets of gold and a sea of crystal. It is something that no human intelligence can build or

## INTRODUCTION

imagine; it is the New Jerusalem with its imposing beauty, a paradise prepared for me and you.

Would you like to know how you can transform your life and convince yourself that there is still hope and something great prepared for you? Come with me. I will take you along that wide path that I walked, which became a path in the middle of chaos, to reach a place full of hope and joy.

Suppose you believe that your story of defeat is not over yet. Still, you require a powerful force from above to help you overcome adversity and rise like a mighty eagle to other heights so that from there, you can be free from all your battles and emerge victorious. In that case, I ask you to follow me and come closer to my story, you will understand that in just an instant your life can change completely. Then, you will know that all your struggles do not compare to that joy that fills everything in your life. Come back Home! That is, your life will take you from victory to victory

# 1
# Dreaming of a path to freedom

The last 25 years of my existence have been a long and deep journey in search of "a better life," a radical transformation to become a better version of myself. The good thing about this, dear reader, is that you do not have to suffer all these years to transform your life. Your change can be as fast as accepting that there is a better way that leads us to victory.

All my years before finding my longed-for purpose in life were about following my paths without understanding that I had to advance along God's paths. Advance under His will and not my own.

I thought I had to live in constant evolution in the world, always striving to reach a higher level in my personal life, more material wealth, more excellent learning in business, and more economic achievements. Because of this way of thinking and acting, I forgot I did not need to transform to scale more objectives constantly.

What I really needed was to remember who the Creator and Author of my life is. I never thought that what I most aspired to in the deepest part of my being would be revealed to me very amazingly. Even though the wait seemed like an eternity, the encounter, the miracle, happened instantly. So remember: the light will always come.

I would never have thought that my existence could hold that magnitude of transformation as it has been in the last two years. Suddenly, I realized I was looking for little things and had found a bigger prize. Yes, a new pact, a new life, a new rebirth!

Well, when I could SEE what was in my mind, face to face, everything changed in my life. The steps I have taken have been plodding at times, although suddenly, some come that seem to reach great speed. And in all this time, I must have had a lot of patience and great faith.

Of course, I always remember my final destination, aware that He offers us His great splendor, His light to welcome His people. As I advanced slowly and precisely, I heard a voice that told me, "You took a sure step, now you must take another…" and so it has happened until this moment when I can tell you about the process of this beautiful and inexplicable encounter with God.

Some stories of transformation sometimes seem resplendent, imposing, and incredible, where various people offer the "how" to change habits, destinies, life projects, or stories of famous people or politicians who tell how they lost everything, failed in their businesses and became bankrupt and suddenly regained success, recovered their wealth, even increased it.

We also know of very expensive programs where people pay thousands of dollars to help them lose weight, have a healthy family relationship, achieve financial success, and create successful businesses; programs that ask for help so that they give us a direction to achieve health and well-being in our lives without realizing that those who are supposed to provide us with that help do not even know where they are or where they are going.

They believe they can transform other lives and raise people's self-esteem, and they feel precious. Let me tell you that all of these are traps of this deceitful world with characters who only want to entangle you in lies and falsehood, who offer you physical and spiritual salvation, and who only manage, sometimes, to share temporary joys.

**It seems that we live in a time of many mysteries, although there are also those of us who believe that there are no such mysteries but rather a certainty that something will come, something that perhaps our human mind cannot understand. However, on the spiritual plane, we know that someone great with power and all his glory will come, and all eyes will see it.**

Every day, more and more people present themselves as coaches, trainers, teachers, lecturers, speakers, content creators, and influencers. They tell you that they can help you achieve your goals, motivate you to fulfill your life purpose, and help you rise from all your falls to have a full, happy, abundant, successful life.

In today's world, there is a great need to feel fulfilled and fill our life gaps. Every day, we see people running from one place to another in search of filling those huge gaps that torment them. At the same time, there is a great need for people to be heard and guided on the path of "the truth" that is so much talked about.

And yes, it seems that many have the answer because there are countless people who offer answers to discouragement and sadness, many who promise good physical and mental health, but unfortunately, many of these people who offer you a life of achievements and satisfaction do not offer anything transcendent or true.

There are already too many books today that promise to solve all your problems or show you the way to achieve your goals, and every day, more books are added to the market on these topics; to this, we must add that those interested sometimes take a course and believe that they have already found the great secret to achieving success in their undertaking, adequate progress in one of their goals, but what they get is so little, only a part of the growth, of the encounter, and this does not guarantee that they will prosper in their entire search, in their long journey.

That is why we should not let ourselves be fooled by everything they promise us, with false strategies of happiness and even gospels of prosperity, because even more things will come that will divert us from the path Home. The more we look for the short "express" routes of transformation, the more we will experience situations of doubt, even pain, that we will have to heal. The more you search the world for the solution to your emotional imbalances, the more tragedies and conflicts you will find; you will always have difficult situations or dark times as long as you do not see the path back Home.

I will not talk to you about those kinds of transformations that are talked about a lot on social media and in the world of material wealth, about all that healing your wounds through motivations and speeches that are only words and not facts, because they are not the best to relieve the feeling of emptiness you have.

We already know that in these times, the noise of information prevails, the false promises, the cry of those who claim to have the

## 1. DREAMING OF A PATH TO FREEDOM

truth, all this noise makes it difficult to hear clearly, to understand where the truth we need is and the path we must follow to return Home. Therefore, based on my experience, I will talk to you about what actual failure is, defeat in life, and I will tell you how to get up to achieve true success, the triumph that any human being can achieve.

Now, I can confess that many years of my life had been a farce, a lie. I only pretended to be a very successful woman (although I was, inside, I felt like a failure), a woman who motivated everyone but me because I felt lost; I couldn't have joy or security anywhere. That supposed success I had was not the triumph I wanted, I also thought that I had not come to the world for something as small as that, and temporary. I thought I had come to the world for something bigger and more powerful, to search with my senses awake for something eternal, to bear witness to it and spread it across the globe.

When I began searching to become a "better version" of "myself," I took into my hands any book within reach related to prosperity, motivation, and how to create businesses. And I was successful. But there came a time when I realized that everything I was achieving did not fill that vast and deep void I had. I even felt that it was getting more profound and more painful. I realized that my feelings regarding my search and activities were becoming more evident and empty. I no longer only felt that emptiness that affected my spiritual, physical, and emotional life. Something powerful was growing with that emptiness that became an excruciating and large wound, which grew daily and deepened, touching other layers of my soul and causing more loneliness and pain.

With this emptiness and the wound, the only thing certain was suffering, and I only numbed my wounds with useless material things. I filled my mind with studies of hollow philosophies and information on how to have successful businesses, which only temporarily covered my wounds. Still, the only thing I managed to do was deceive myself. I believed I would become a wise woman by reading all these kinds of books, but I was totally wrong.

Later, I learned that what I needed was to expand my horizons, rise higher, much higher, above all my apparent achievements, successes, and also my falls, bad habits, and failures, and recognize that I was a genuinely ignorant and foolish woman. That all I was doing was feeding my ego. I would not just rise above my faults but become a humble and even ignorant woman so that something supernatural would happen, and from there, the return Home would take place to obtain true victory.

The actual endpoint for me, and I hope it can be for you - is to understand that we must begin to walk like newborn children and be willing to beg the Wonderful, Counselor, Mighty God, Eternal Father, Prince of Peace, or whatever you want to call him, to teach us to walk, to speak, to think and to look to obtain true wisdom: to be a sensible person from above and not with earthly wisdom marked by ego and presumption, because that is only temporary; to be a person truly dedicated to a mission that offers eternal fruits, a reward that has been granted to us by divine inheritance. I must say that I am not a wise woman, as I mistakenly believed myself to be. Every day, I prostrate myself before His holy presence as an ignorant woman to ask Him to make me a humble and noble woman, to help me cross

## 1. DREAMING OF A PATH TO FREEDOM

the daily path, and to offer help and not obstacles to those who have not found the way back Home.

Now I recognize it: I was wrong for many years. I believed that true prosperity was to be wealthy and successful. But everything changed when I returned Home and understood that to prosper in life we must do much more than create a business and accumulate wealth, we must bow down every morning before His divine presence and let Him guide us: may it always be His will and not ours. I love learning the meaning of words, and I knew that the word "prosperity" in "Hebrew means "to make way" or "an inspiring push" to evolve.

We have to learn how to advance in our lives with a divine plan that God has for each of us, for all His people, and not a plan we make. Sometimes, we create something and think it is the perfect plan. But His Word says that His plans are not our plans. It may hurt us to admit it, but it is a great truth. There is no other perfect plan than God's Word, which says that He already knew us before the foundation of the world. He already had that perfect plan for my life and yours. Do not look for that plan anymore. You will not find it; on the contrary, what will most likely happen to you is what happened to me: instead of seeing my perfect plan, I arrived at muddy lakes. Remember: the ideal plan was already made for you. You have to immerse yourself in the essence of Him in its entirety, full-time, not only when it suits you, and stop relying on hollow philosophies that, in the end, only offer confusion and a great emptiness for our lives.

**In these pages, I will try to tell you about something much greater than all those conventional philosophies and discourses that I learned and lived for years. I will tell you about di-**

**vine power, miracles, and supernatural power and its wonderful mysteries that can reach you in the blink of an eye and completely change your life.**

You won't have time to ask yourself so many questions about why and what for; you will only realize that you no longer live in darkness! Then you will be free from all ties, and from there, there is no turning back because the light you find is admirable and so excellent that you will only be attentive, looking forward and upward, waiting for something even more remarkable to come. You can achieve that if you return Home and allow God to work supernaturally to recognize that I am about to get too vulnerable right now.

I want to mention something to you before continuing because, throughout this book, I will say some things that may make you uncomfortable. You may think this does not happen to everyone, much less to you. Therefore, it will not be able to help you get up from your failures and falls. When these "different" things are mentioned in these pages that you have not heard, seen, or felt, or if you have heard them, you have ignored them; I tell you now with all respect that this is your great opportunity to read something genuinely supernatural and transformative that can lead you to a life experience that you have never experienced. The best way to begin is to think with your end in mind; that is, think about how you feel the last day of your life will be.

Will it be worth it to have the awareness that you only live once and lose the opportunity for something eternal? What will become of our coming years, and after we finish our career on earth, what will happen to our souls? Because if you think that you are going through

## 1. DREAMING OF A PATH TO FREEDOM

tough times, I am sorry to tell you that difficult times will still come. Are you prepared?

My only significant purpose in this book is to tell you what happened in my life to go from a confused existence, without direction, with severe depression, empty and in a total, devastating crisis, as if I lived in a frozen and dark desert without any protection, to my search for God, his light and his promises that are still valid, with his loving hope in which we can rest our lives confidently.

To reveal to you what made me hit rock bottom and begin to reflect on the kind of life I had that was not worth it and how my life was transformed through a supernatural event that touched me deeply so that I could leave the darkness and go to his beautiful light because it was with that miracle that my life changed completely.

I will share with you the testimony of all my failures, losses, bad habits, apparent successes, and achievements that never relieved my emptiness. I will tell you where I came from where I am now and what I still hope to receive from the moment I had that sign and did not hesitate for a second to accept His call, the presence of the Almighty that fills everything and told me with an indescribable warmth: "Come down," like in the Bible story where Jesus tells Zacchaeus: "Hurry, come down, for today I must stay at your house," Luke 19:5 (NKJV). So I had that second chance to return Home so He could control my life.

Now I am back Home, and I want to tell you about the process of moving forward. I want to plant a seed in your life and walk with you so that you, too, can allow God to transform your life with his power and help you get out of that path that is so difficult for you but that you cannot abandon, where you keep trying to open paths, doors, and if they open you only run into walls. I lived that moment, so do not waste your precious time. There is another better path where you do not have to face that enormous force of opening locks and undoing many chains to open doors. Stop doing that! Choose the narrow path of God that the world does not know because it follows with total freedom the wide path, without limits and full of superficiality, without paying attention to what they do.

I will tell you about that broad path that led me to the narrow path where one truly goes from victory to victory. I will also tell you what my life is like today, what I aspire to, and what sustains me. I will tell you how a seed planted in me a few years ago became a fountain of living water that refreshes my soul. That same seed is what I want to place in you through my story, to plant it in your heart so that one day it will be transformed, and you can benefit from the "milk and honey" that God has prepared for your life.

If you wish, today can be a great day for your life; if you are a person who has tried everything in life and does not find satisfaction with only your earthly triumphs, if you struggle to feel emotionally fulfilled and only live overwhelmed by your present, with the feeling that there is something that is not right in that place where you live (in your current world) because you feel that you should be doing something much more powerful with your life, but you do not find the answers to what you are looking for, perhaps today you will have certainty in these pages, a sign of His admirable light to take that significant step towards a new life. A transformed life.

## 1. DREAMING OF A PATH TO FREEDOM

I am sure that if you read my testimony, you will find a sign, and there, amid your tribulations, from that place of doubts and worries where you may be and where everything seems confusing, without finding a way out, you will suddenly find the answer, the place where you belong. You will have a sign and see a tiny light that will be enough to take a step forward. You may already know what I will tell you, but you do not yet have the foundation of that solid Home.

Sometimes, you feel that the dwelling is too old, outdated, uninhabitable, and needs a good remodel. Get ready! I will tell you how to live in that beautiful house again and feel like you are in that mansion you are stepping on. I will never stop revealing how wonderful it feels to express what I am experiencing. I will always thank God for allowing me to go through this desert, lost and with a great thirst so that He could wake me up from that suffering and take me out of the muddy path where I was delivered and take me to His house so that I could witness that definitive moment in which He told me: "Up to here; now get up, you are in my hands, let me mold you in my way, and thus your life will be transformed." It seems like this happened an eternity ago, and in just the blink of an eye, His infinite glory was manifested in my life.

So, no matter what situation you are in now, no matter how great your burdens, doubts, difficulties, or how lost or disoriented you feel in life if you do not know whether to go left, right, forward, or backward, in reality, none of that matters. Even if your life is in permanent darkness, and you have lost faith, you should rejoice because something great wants to penetrate your life.

The biggest fear I had in my life was ending my days lost in unknown lands, lost, just as I was in my world of chaos and darkness, ending up as a foreigner feeling like I was not in the right place for me where I could live in fullness, a place where I did not fit in and with experiences of failure and fear with the idea that my life would come to an end at any moment—yes, living in a vicious circle.

Sometimes, we spend our lives in trial and error to improve, but nothing happens. On the other hand, sometimes an unusual event appears in the blink of an eye, like a supernatural miracle that comes like a lightning bolt, a short circuit that illuminates everything and completely transforms existence to convince you that your life will never be the same. Yes. It is the presence of God.

# 2

# The path of rebellion

Before I continue, I want to tell you some things I experienced firsthand that have defined my way of understanding life until today.

And if there is one thing that has become very clear to me, it is that bad decisions have their consequences, but they do not have to define your future.

I want this book to reach the deepest part of your heart and not be just another book like the ones you have read.

This is not a motivational book to help you with your self-esteem, nor is it a book to help you be successful in business, or a book of personal development like those that abound and promise you happiness and success in all areas of your life; I am not going to tell you that you are a Superman or Super-woman who can achieve everything your mind imagines and that while you read these pages, you will have a great motivation to devour the world, even if this impulse disappears after a few days, that desire to achieve and conquer dies.

This happened to me many times with those books I read for years. At first, I believed in their motivations, rules, and recipes, but then a great disappointment arose because everything seemed like a mirage, a fantasy. Everything became meaningless, empty phrases that did not reach the depths of my heart. And if some of them did get me, they were only for a while, without achieving any change in my life. All that motivational information disappeared after a few days.

I want you to see this book as a testimony of life or death. And yes, maybe it feels a little exaggerated, but the transformation I experienced could not be expressed in any other way. Because I insist it was something supernatural that happened to me. I could free myself from all the ties and dangers I saw coming into my life because my existence was fading away; it was going away in seconds. One day I even experienced how my spirit left my body, and I felt that at that moment I no longer belonged to this world of colors, aromas, of joy and movement, of searching!, that I had already died.

The wonderful thing is that that day I did not understand everything precisely because many things were happening to me, and I could not perceive all this reality well; I was totally in the dark, without seeing the light, in a deep darkness that suffocated me and enveloped me, I was spiritually dead all those years without the divine presence of HIM! But now, something was warning me that I could descend even lower, go into free fall downwards, and still, the light could be revealed in my life. And so it was precisely, I was able to look at his admirable light when I was in the bottomless abyss, I was able to see it once again and forever, and here I am to tell you about its wonders.

## 2. THE PATH OF REBELLION

I want to be as honest as possible with you. I want to tell you about my search, abysses, and encounter with Him. That is why I believe this book is a tool that tries to help you get out of the great path of confusion and doubts you find yourself on, out of that sad stagnation. It tries to help you get out of that desert and darkness to direct yourself towards a path that may be very narrow and difficult to walk, but that is worth it to reach HIM. Today, I can assure you: if He did something extraordinary in my life, He will do it in yours too.

On that narrow path, you will experience what it means to have "true success in life," that promise of happiness that we sometimes achieve but only momentarily, because that is how the earthly realm is; but on a spiritual level, we understand that none of the earthly achievements or material things will fill that void where most of this world is currently. Because human nature brings that emptiness from the beginning of humanity, but when divine illumination comes into our lives, everything changes. We no longer live in darkness.

**Sometimes, we are baffled when we believe achieving success is having victory, but that is not the case. Success can be measured by your external earnings, professional titles, material possessions, money, houses, businesses, investments... But victory is something much more profound and of incalculable value; it is more powerful and eternal. Victory is over our fears, doubts and insecurities, and it is achieved through faith and trust, and even if we go through tribulations, we know that we are not alone in these battles, God has the power to undo any trap that wants to trap us.**

I must also tell you that if you want something supernatural to work and transform your life, you must have a spirit of courage and self-control, be convinced of what you are looking for to act at the right time, and have the humility to bend and let God enter your life and be the one who guides you and faces your battles, only then will you be able to aspire to be a winner and obtain victory. Furthermore, I assure you, Jesus will not leave you as He found you but will transform your life entirely as He did with me.

"No one will be able to stand against you all the days of your life; as I was with Moses so that I will be with you; I will not leave or forsake you. Be strong and courageous, for you will give this people the land I swore to their fathers to give to them as an inheritance. Only be strong and very courageous, to be careful to do according to all the law that my servant Moses commanded you; Do not turn from it to the right or the left, so that you may prosper in whatever you do," Joshua 1:5-7 (NKJV): this promise is valid for your life and my life.

Maybe you even experienced suicide attempts; perhaps you wished you had never been born; you suffered terrible anxiety, a depression that at some point you thought would lead to your death; maybe you felt invisible or unable to conceive; you felt that your life was the most bitter and painful loneliness. I understand you perfectly because I felt that way. Empty, sad, and in the most immense desolation you can imagine. But be confident that if you look for HIM, a miracle will come into your life, and you will be free. God will take your life, which seems like a puzzle, and turn it into a masterpiece and an irrevocable miracle.

Now, I will continue with this chapter, and I want to tell you that there is great symbolism in the fact of being or leaving Home. In

## 2. THE PATH OF REBELLION

these times, there are times when parents allow their children to go out of the house when they do not obey the rules of the Home; in this scenario, they believe that the most convenient thing is for them to go out so that they learn to be responsible and good children so that they discover that life outside the Home is not easy, on the contrary, it is full of obligations, conflicts, and challenges. A lack of guidance leads them to make mistakes and commit numerous errors, sometimes straightforward, typical of their age, and without severe consequences. Still, they can also be terrible ones that lead to tragedies.

When I lived in my country, Mexico, during my childhood, those situations were very different from those we live in now. In those days, you were left alone at Home so that you could learn to be responsible, take care of yourself and your younger siblings, and even be the head of the house to take care of her.

I remember one time when I was 8 or 10 years old, I was listening to my mother and my older sister chatting very entertainingly without them noticing my presence; they were talking about their plans to leave the house, do some shopping, or they were organizing themselves for a walk. This was a sign that I would stay Home to do and undo as I pleased. Listening to their conversation was very exciting because instead of getting sad, I would be left alone. With some work left to me while they were out, I was excited because I could play, eat, and do whatever I wanted without scolding or supervision. It made me so happy that I helped them prepare quickly so they could leave the house as soon as possible and finally be alone.

Nowadays, times are very different, and people do not usually leave children alone at Home when they go shopping or out for fun.

Still, in my childhood in a beautiful town in Mexico, this situation was prevalent and, at least in my case, sometimes the older ones went out for a walk or to do some activity that had to do with work or daily obligations and left the younger ones at Home, it was also possible that someone older among the children took care of the other younger children, and that was my case, but why was it exciting for me to leave my mother's and my sister's house? Because I loved playing with my friends at Home without anyone stopping us from doing what we wanted, because I would wear my older sister's shoes, clothes and accessories and even if they didn't fit me, I felt incredible, wearing her things was fascinating for a girl full of dreams like me.

Whether I was meeting up with some friends or alone, my imagination was overflowing, and I loved making messes all over the house that almost looked like a hurricane had passed. And then I had to clean up before they came back, hurry up with the mess I had made! And to my surprise, there were times when they came back early, and I got into serious trouble, then my joy turned into tears, the scoldings and punishments, although perhaps not so great for my few years, were terrible, and I suffered a lot.

I don't know if you have identified with my story or if you ever went through something similar in which you disobeyed or created such a mess that your parents punished you, and you still remember it to this day; the truth is that it is very tempting when we have moments of freedom because we mess up, we believe ourselves independent and capable of everything, and we don't think about the consequences. I guess that happens when you get involved in the now and not the tomorrow. For example, do you remember when you

## 2. THE PATH OF REBELLION

were in high school, and you would skip classes to leave school with your friends and enjoy walking around the city, having fun walking through the streets, going to some recreational place, or maybe looking for a place to eat ice cream? I was happy to be with my friends, to live that moment with them, but what about the consequences if the teachers accused us of our parents if I didn't show up for an exam or didn't do my homework because of these pranks that are also indiscipline? Harsh consequences, right?

Something vital occurs when we leave our place of origin—our home, the neighborhood we live in, and even our comfort zone. This departure can be dangerous because we drift away from what is considered "correct." As we move further from divine law and truth, we distance ourselves from our true selves and our environment, from the nurturing shelter that provides safety. This journey can lead us to face significant challenges, moments of confusion, disorder, and anguish as we stray from our essence. However, something extraordinary happens when we return home; we regain our sense of harmony.

It is very different from when we are away from Home because doubt and disorganization prevail even though we want everything under control. If you analyze a little more carefully, you will realize that even when you are planning a vacation, whether for a short or long time, you are filled with joy, you start your plans, you are super happy with them, you make some purchases to have the necessary changes of clothes, new shoes and the night before your departure you can't even sleep because of the excitement…

But what happens when a few days or months pass after your trip? Maybe you feel very agitated; that excitement is probably not like the first days; you may feel sick, tired, and frustrated, sometimes you miss your Home, and you want to return to it regardless of whether during your trip you were staying in a five-star hotel and the Home, that awaits you, is a tiny house without many luxuries, but that is the Home where you feel safe and pleased!

Why do I say this? This simple example confirms that, even if I can surround myself with riches, lavish comforts, luxuries, the most advanced technologies, or money, if my search has no light, any place, no matter how wonderful it may seem, will be incomplete. Do you agree that an expensive hotel, with abundant food and drink and dazzling suites, does not work for well-being if it has no light or if darkness and mistrust prevail?

Now I want to tell you something that also happened to me when I was a child. Maybe I was eight or nine years old, and I was happy playing in the vegetation of the place where I grew up. I lived in a humble rural area of Mexico, and on that occasion, I found myself hanging from a lemon tree on a beautiful sunset. I loved climbing trees, swinging, and playing among the branches.

At that time, I felt happy among the leaves and the gentle murmur of the wind. While swinging from side to side on the tree, I listened intently to the conversation my older sister was having with our cousin. They talked about parties, trips, boys, and the fun that young people have. I paid close attention to their discussion, absorbing every detail while my imagination raced a thousand miles an hour, envisioning the places, encounters, and experiences they were describing.

Suddenly, I interrupted their conversation because I found it incoherent; none of the things they were discussing or wishing for

## 2. THE PATH OF REBELLION

made much sense to me. I told them that nothing they wanted caught my interest; instead, I yearned to travel far away and explore many places. I even mentioned my desire to go to the Middle East and shared all the details of what I wanted to do there, speaking like a girl full of dreams. They looked at me with wide eyes, as if to say, "Where did this girl come from? Where is she headed? Is she just daydreaming?"

Annoyed because I was listening to them and thinking I was crazy for everything I told them, they asked me to leave there, not to listen to adult conversations. They were shocked because what I told them came from the soul. So, I slowly climbed down from the lemon tree, and thinking about everything I had heard and what I had told them, I walked away from there and reflected on my future. I wondered how I would answer so many questions that arose about what the purpose of my life really would be and when the time would come for me to detach myself towards the beyond, towards the heights, what would be the moment when I would begin a long adventure of my life without imagining where or when the endpoint would arrive.

Now that I think about it, I know that at that time, I did not know geography, much less what the Middle East was, nor did I know where it was because there was no television at Home. It seemed as if climbing those trees where I loved to climb had caused me "air sickness" because, since my childhood, my life had never been "normal." I always dreamed and always wanted to become the best possible version of myself, and although I did not know much about God and my faith was not well-founded in HIM, when I was little, I had not immersed myself in his divinity, in the "Elohim," in the supreme, in the almighty; However, I did feel that there was something to do and that no one would do it for me, I felt a calling that I had to obey.

**Later, I realized that I had to accept this call from the depths of my soul, that God was giving me a new opportunity to follow his command, light, and guidance. If, for a long time, I had made mistakes and had chosen paths of superficiality, dazzled by material things, the traps of the ego, and false proposals of spiritual well-being, now, after many setbacks, I had to be humble and thank the call, the luminous invitation to return to the shelter of God.**

Today, when I remember that childhood experience, I think that all those times I swung from the branches of the trees were like a sign that I would go from one place to another, from north to south and from east to west. This indicated to me that this would be my future: traveling from one place to another, in many directions, I would move through many places without a fixed course to rest my soul.

When I swung from the trees, I will tell you how those thoughts among the branches went from being glances at the sky. The leaves with flashes, shadows, and lemon tree aromas to trips outside my town, outside my city and Mexico, visits to the Middle East, to Iran, a place that a nine-year-old girl spoke of without knowing it, and that would become a fantastic reality. Today, I can quote the following: "The sun is for everyone, but the shadow of the Almighty is only for those who decided to enter the shelter of the Most High." Psalm 91:1.

# 3

# A new pact for a transformative encounter

In 1989, I bravely and at a young age, decided to leave my country to immigrate to the United States. I was just a teenager, almost a child, when I left my town in Mexico without knowing how the world revolved around me. I was barely 14 years old, but despite my young age, I had high expectations for my future without even imagining how I would cross deserts and deserts.

I came from a humble, very conservative, and "Catholic" family. However, we did not practice religion and only used that name to say that we had a belief because I never really knew what it was like to be a fully dedicated Catholic. At a young age, I never had a strong connection with the church, and before moving forward, I apologize to Catholic readers if some of my words make them feel bad; at no time is that my intention; I only want to express my search; this is my story, and I want to tell it as it was, with absolute sincerity, without adding or taking anything away.

During my childhood, I remember attending catechism a few months before making my First Communion, and I will never forget the occasion when I had to be confessed by the Catholic Church priest as a requirement to make my Communion.

I remember that I had to prostrate myself at his feet to "confess my sins" at that young age, but in the mind of that girl that I was, I did not know what was going on around me. I felt I had no sins because I did not do bad things; the only thing I did every day was play with my friends and have fun without bothering anyone. However, the father told me: "My daughter, confess all your sins." At that moment, I looked around to see if I could find my mother, perhaps with the desire for her to save me, to rescue me from that test that I did not fully understand, but it distressed me; I did not know what to say, and I just wanted to burst into tears, then the father insisted "daughter, I am waiting for you to confess your sins." At that moment, I thought that to get out of that interrogation, I would have to invent "some sin," and so I did.

A fearful voice came out of my mouth that was cut off by worry, and I told him that my sins were that lately, I had killed many little birds; it occurred to me that because I climbed trees and played in the fields, that was my world and having fun among the branches and the meadows was my passion. That was the only thing that came to my mind, and I remained silent, waiting for the priest to punish me.

I felt terrified, but I was ready to accept any punishment that they gave me. Then the priest told me in a powerful, powerful voice that I will never forget: "Daughter, you are a sinner; go to the altar and kneel to ask for forgiveness; you must pray these prayers…" He ordered me to say a series of prayers that I did not understand; I only remember that I got on my knees and began to feel guilty for saying

## 3. A NEW PACT FOR A TRANSFORMATIVE ENCOUNTER

something that I should not have said, although the events forced me to do so, to come out of my innocence and to think from that age that perhaps the priest should have asked me more things and noticed my anguish and not just punished as a method. Then I blamed my mother because I had to confess sins that I did not have, sins that I had not committed nor did I consider having at my young age, and that made me feel that I was worthless. She remained silent and was never able to answer me.

Since I was a little girl, I always asked many questions about things in life for which I could not find an answer or explanation. I was always like that; I questioned everything, worried myself, and went to my mother to ask. It seemed that from the moment I came into this world, I came prepared with many questions to ask whoever was before me about the why and wherefore of life. It seemed I was designated to uncover many hidden things and reveal situations that were not yet discovered.

By searching and finding answers to my questions, I would have to testify and share what I learned. That would be what would mark my life from the beginning, to recognize the purpose for which I came here and navigate through life so that my pain would deepen, to die in life and return to live to travel the only authentic path to carry out the GREAT COMMISSION and that will lead us to receive the grand prize. Over the years, I understood that the time had come for me to leave on a long journey full of experiences, pains, and lessons and that one day, I would finally return to a place prepared just for me.

How can I forget that afternoon, very close to dusk, after finishing washing a lot of clothes by hand and while I was starting to hang them on the clothesline to dry, my mother approached me and asked me if I would like to go live in the United States with my brothers. Without thinking twice, I quickly answered: "Of course! What day do I leave?" "Now that I think about it, I believe that I have been like that since I was a child: determined and fearless, willing to do anything to improve my quality of life. It seemed that that evening, as I took one garment after another to hang them to dry, I was taking those clothes in my hands as a symbol of protection. With them, I tried to cover my soul because I felt so spiritually naked at a young age that I wanted a protective shell and wings to feel safe so that all the doubts I had would not lead me to spiritual suicide.

And so it happened…

When I was still a little girl, I told my parents, "I'm leaving next week." "And although inside, I felt terror about everything that could happen in my life, I pretended to be very sure of what I was doing since I was a child, as I already said, and they saw me with eyes that showed me I was very sure of myself and firm for everything I would have to face in life. But nobody knew that I was full of insecurities, nerves, and questions without answers.

I didn't know everything I had to go through to get to the United States, but my ambitions were grand. I never thought about the consequences of leaving for another place, not only outside my town but also from my country to another world. I left my house with only a change of clothes in a small bag one of my neighbor's friends gave me.

Almost naked, I left Home with that small luggage, full of fears and dreams. The clothes were nearly nothing, minimal, but I felt full of faith, ambitions, and a great desire to explore another world to

## 3. A NEW PACT FOR A TRANSFORMATIVE ENCOUNTER

answer the many questions I had at that young age. Since I can remember, I have always thought that there is something more than walking through this earth without a fixed direction, without reason, or without knowing where to go; I believe that there must be something much more significant in the afterlife because life cannot be just arriving here to go to school, work and get married; I knew that there was something more, something supernatural that small human minds cannot perceive, it takes enormous faith to feel that incredible and invisible presence.

So I embarked towards a new country that, for me, would be the beginning of new horizons, where I not only had to cross the border like many immigrants who come to this country in search of a better life, but in my case, I never imagined that I would have to leave my land to get here and begin to walk in a desert to return Home, where I truly belong finally.

**Now I know that truly our Home is not only the place of birth, but the place where everything will be revealed to you, and that does not happen when we are in a place where we do not belong; we receive the keys to our Home when we accept His call when we accept that He guides us and that He always does His will in everything we undertake.**

So we must not underestimate anything in the search nor complain when walking tired in the desert, thirsty, and sometimes even lost because we are disoriented. At the same time, we cross that dry land towards other new horizons where everything will happen: falls, setbacks, disasters, great tragedies, and defeats, but it is there, in that suffering and desolation, where the light and victory arrive.

Never forget, the light will always arrive.

Can you imagine me when I was 14 years old and was going to cross the border? I entered a country that was unknown to me; I did not have a solid foundation of faith in God, either. I remember that I only heard that the world would end very soon in those years. I never knew what it was like to have an approach to God and to entrust my path to Him. I was at a point in my life when I only knew that I was going to cross the border into a country whose language I did not know, the culture, much less what other houses of God there were to get closer to HIM and have a genuine relationship with my creator.

I remember that, among the many things I went through to cross the border, I suddenly found myself inside a considerable truck surrounded by men and women. There, a girl who was in charge of that group of people who were inside approached me. She extraordinarily stared at me, then she approached me and began to touch me inappropriately. I started to feel very confused about what was happening. I was just a teenager with the innocence of a child. I came from a town, from a province. I had never seen such things in my life. I had only heard from a priest from the parish of my city that I was a sinner, and for me, it was terrible. But at that moment, in front of that woman, I was experiencing something genuinely frightening.

Thoughts of desperation, anger, disappointment, and a massive lack of ability to defend myself from something that felt horrible ran through my brain. The journey seemed eternal to me until I crossed the border. I came with a feeling of fear and distrust. I could not imagine what awaited me in the new country. I had to start a new

## 3. A NEW PACT FOR A TRANSFORMATIVE ENCOUNTER

world, learn the language, learn new ways to interact with people, and make friends; yes, I had to start from scratch.

Here I want to tell you something that I would like to stick in your mind and that you will never forget: maybe you are sad because of things that have happened in your life, harrowing things that you have had to face, bad experiences, disappointments, failures, sufferings that seem to lead you to death; you should know that there is a God who has been recording every act of your life step by step, HE has been taking note of everything to reward you for everything you have gone through, suffered, endured in your bitterest days. Remember: "I will restore to you the years that the caterpillar has eaten, the canker worm, the canker worm, and the locust, My great army which I sent among you." Joel 2:25 (NKJV).

It is undoubtedly a beautiful promise. You have not lost anything; everything will be multiplied to you and given to you from the beginning with interest. I never thought that God would make paths in my life in places where I never thought it's possible to find them, and up to this moment, HE continues to guide me and open doors in my path.

Now, I will tell you about my first encounter with God, an encounter full of eternal promises, not as the world shares them in a superficial way. God's promises are full of hope that will light up my life because He is faithful and merciful.

As I confessed to you, I arrived in the United States alone, without my parents and almost a child, with the traumatic experience of nearly being abused on the bus in which we crossed the border. I feel deeply alone, with many insecurities and a lack of guidance to direct me, to orient me in this new life entire of new things and complications; despite this, my hopes and desire for improvement did not decline as happens to many of us who immigrate and arrive in this country.

Sometimes, I think that by being so often lulled by those trees of my childhood, by being rocked so many times on those strong branches, perhaps I have been prepared to take other paths; I have been strengthened to move in the face of dangers with decision, with courage and thus detach myself with strength to fly very far, very high, and prepare myself for a tremendous and surprising transformative encounter for my life. I know that God sometimes puts us in unknown places for a particular purpose; HE works in a way that no master mind can ever understand its mysteries.

After asking myself so many questions all the time and a long journey with experiences that marked my life, suddenly, one day, I found myself at the doors of an apostolic house of worship. I felt that I had arrived in the Promised Land; the moment had come when I could quench my soul from so much thirst, not only for the trip and my decisions, but also for a thirst that I carried for years of living in "a dry land".

There, my soul could be filled with rivers of living water that ran towards me. Thus, a joy was born that I had never felt before. I am not lying to you if I tell you that I felt afraid of what had come to me at some point, and I did not understand how to cope with it.

Have you had drastic changes that you may not know how to explain, and have you kept those emotions a secret? Have you thought briefly about how God works in your life inexplicably and miracu-

## 3. A NEW PACT FOR A TRANSFORMATIVE ENCOUNTER

lously? Think about it carefully. So when you go through any dark change in your life, never complain to God or ask Him why. Instead, ask Him why, ask what you want me to do with all the changes you are going through, and remember: nothing is by chance.

God had to take me from my birthplace so that I could come to know Him and have the opportunity to find the answers to all my questions. It wasn't before I felt that he had called me to serve Him and do His will. I heard His message of redemption and His beautiful words of love that gave me comfort and peace of mind that everything was going to be okay, as well as words of hope for a better life, and that message reached the depths of my heart because that was precisely what I was looking for! Since I was very young, I felt a vast emptiness in my life.

I could only hear a voice that told me that I had to give Him all my worries, desires, goals, and whole life so that He could take me like a clay vessel and make me His way. He asked me to give Him all my faults, sufferings, anguish, and longings, and if I gave Him my life, this would allow Him to enter mine. I was anxious and hungry for the word of God, so I gave my life to Christ and was baptized in the name of Jesus Christ for the forgiveness of my sins, and I felt liberated.

I was new to this country, the United States. I had to assimilate the customs and the language, and, at the same time, I had a transcendental encounter with faith in God that I did not have in my country. What was happening to me seemed terrific: living in new lands, learning a new language and a new covenant: "One Lord, one faith, and one baptism." That was what my life needed. I was turning away from my faithless past and beginning a new life. Perhaps this is why these words have such significant meaning for me: "Therefore if anyone is in Christ, he is a new creation; old things have passed away; behold, all things have become new" 2 Corinthians 5:17 (NKJV)

When I gave my life to Christ and heard this verse from the Bible, I was not only filled with excitement for all the things revealed, but I also felt a lot of fear for what my new life would be like and how I would lead it with these mysteries, this new path that was opening up for me. I implored myself: Another new life? It seemed that I was afraid of beginning a new cycle in my existence, and more than that, I was scared of failing the promise I had made.

Everything happening to me was perfect and promising, with a bright future and a glorious ending. Still, because of the fear that took hold of me at that moment, I made a huge mistake: I did not ask God to give me a spirit of discernment to have the ability to choose what was healthy for me and what was damaging my spiritual life.

If we want to receive something from God, we must ask Him and never forget: "Ask, and it will be given to you; seek, and you will find; knock, and it will be opened to you." Matthew 7:7 (NKJV). It is true that only in this way will we receive His guidance on what He wants us to do. Because otherwise, we will be living under our own will, and that is when we choose paths that are not God's, and danger can lurk.

I will tell you something that has to do with the fall and its consequences, just as after a collapse, a rise can come that is more potent than defeat. I was always classified as a strong woman who was not afraid of anything, and nothing seemed complicated to me. Sometimes, I said that I could hurt others, crush them with my words, or

## 3. A NEW PACT FOR A TRANSFORMATIVE ENCOUNTER

make them feel bad because of my intense way of saying things. They even told me that I was insulting and that was not my intention because, to be honest, many of the times that I spoke with that strength and sincerity I hid a lot of fear, insecurity and desire to know if I was acting well. Although I already told you that inside, I felt weak.

The joy I felt in the house of God did not last long; I had a pretty strong fall. Fear and battles against the things of the world dragged me into a current that took me to the bottomless abyss. All of this happened because of the loss of commitment, the lack of faith, and the absence of conviction in not knowing how to look with eyes other than those of humans and believe in what is not seen.

We already know that faith is not something you can touch with your hands, but rather the firm and deep confidence in feeling what we do not see, but we know that it is true because of the revelation that was offered to us: "We are told that faith is the substance of things hoped for and the assurance of things not seen" Hebrews 11:1 (NKJV), and my biggest mistake was starting to listen more carefully to the noises of the world and not to the voice of God. It was as if I wanted to seek God but taking steps toward death!

I stopped paying attention to what He wanted me to do. I forgot that He had brought me from other lands so that through His perfect plan, I would meet Him and heed His call because His call was not just to play, to be just a simple visitor in His house: He wanted me to take possession of His Home severely so that I could preach the good news to the depressed, as His word says. Currently, this verse has become one of my favorite texts: "The Spirit of the Lord God is upon me because the Lord has anointed me; He has sent me to preach good news to the depressed, to come and give freedom to the brokenhearted, to proclaim liberty to the captives, and the opening of the prison to those in prison; to proclaim the year of the lords favor, and the day of vengeance of our God; to comfort all who mourn; to appoint to those who mourn in Zion, to give them glory for ashes, the oil of joy for mourning, the mantle of praise for the spirit of heaviness; and they shall be called trees of righteousness, the planting of the LORD, that he may be glorified" Isaiah 61:1-3 (NKJV).

Every time I think about my true purpose in life, I think I want to always be like a tree of justice, a plantation of Jehovah for his glory. In those years, it was not like that, and it took me more than 20 years to understand my long-sought "purpose" to be convinced of my true calling. I hope that it does not take so many years for you, that you do not let yourself be dragged through the desert (on dry, lifeless land) until you die without any hope. I suffered too much for a long time, but I got up. And here I am to tell you everything and accompany you on this beautiful path.

That time when I lost my way and everything became dark in my life was because I could not bear what had been my responsibility as a good soldier of Christ, and I abandoned everything. I lost everything. I left Home and escaped from what God had prepared for my life. I was too impatient, and now I know things do not happen when we want them to. It is His time and not ours. His time is everything; His times are perfect.

That's right; I did not want to obey Him, and I did not accept being a disciple who went around the world speaking of His word. That was one of my most significant responsibilities as a new creature

## 3. A NEW PACT FOR A TRANSFORMATIVE ENCOUNTER

in Christ. Just as it is for all followers of Jesus, I will never remain silent again! Because disobedience has great significant consequences and the wages of sin is death, remember:

"Look straight ahead without turning back, open your mouth, and move your lips to confess who Yahweh is."

**When you find yourself at a moment where you have already had that green light to move forward if you have already been freed from all ties, you will know that your sins have been washed with His blood, and you no longer have to be paralyzed or take steps back!**

Every day, you must take steps forward and rise as high as you can because that state can be perilous if you do not do so. Not taking a step forward immediately can cause you to stagnate and sink into confusion, and the moment you want to get out of there, it will be in reverse, just like what happened to me.

Never look back in the sense of faith, even if you must return to take something you left behind. Never do it. You no longer belong to that past; focus forward. Do not forget that everything is lovely, and everything from above is only found when you are back Home; if you are currently at Home, reaffirm yourself even more and look forward. Abandoning the call that He has sent you brings excellent consequences. Unfortunately, they are not so good because even if everything looks good on the outside, it is only a farce, as confirmed by the saying, "Not everything that glitters is gold." In this earthly world, full of emptiness, there is a lot of denial and pride in human beings, and sometimes, we do not want to accept that we lead a mediocre life.

# 4

# When earthly riches do not fill the heart

There are times when we want to change the world, the people around us, and the context in which we live without understanding that by thinking about putting order on the outside, we neglect our true mission in life and our calling. This, without a doubt, is very dangerous. If you let yourself be carried away by the currents of the river, you will move away from the purpose that God has prepared for your life, which God already had for you since you were in your mother's womb, and it is a fact that if we ignore it, we will later have to beg for guidance and comfort.

That happened to me: I moved too far away from the divine presence; I moved away from Him and had to start a path of begging and suffering. This led me to confirm that darkness cannot mix with light, just as water and oil cannot mix. So, after understanding it, after understanding what a life full of great merciful promises could be, I looked back and, at that moment, I could no longer see the light.

I was left totally blind, spiritually, with a significant blindfold on my eyes, so tight that I had no chance to look a little and get out of that blackness. I realized that I had left the shadow of his omnipotence and had returned to a life equal to or perhaps worse than the one I had already lived, a life of confusion, lack of purpose, an empty, unhappy life.

I asked my father for my spiritual inheritance very early, very young, like that prodigal son, instead of waiting patiently for his will for me. I ultimately moved away from his presence and told him: "I will leave your house to live my life my way because I feel that I can live out there without you. I will know how to defend myself; I have enough to live and achieve, even squander what I want." Since then, I have wrongly felt He had forgotten me because I no longer heard his voice.

I never stopped to think that if I had to cross foreign lands, it was so that I could take possession of what He had prepared for me so that I could discover the mission He had entrusted to me. He wanted to have an encounter with me and for me to once and for all get to know that great I AM that I had sensed since I was a child and that I so desired to know more about His wonders and His power. I always knew that this life was too small for that great thing that I perceived, to have a passport and reach that promised land, that city called the great Jerusalem. I understood that if He made me leave my land and cross the border, it was because He had something great prepared for my life. He had brought me from far away to teach me His ways, to prepare me for a greater calling and thus experience something tremendous and from the highest.

There, with Him, I had everything. I was under the protection of the Almighty, but I left everything to begin other adventures. The

## 4. WHEN EARTHLY RICHES DO NOT FILL THE HEART

rebellion led me again to cross other unknown lands and long and deserted roads, to dry lands, without life, with many unreal, false visions, although very surprising to me.

Now I understand that at that time, I asked my father for my inheritance very early; I was too ahead when I said: "Father, give me the part of the goods that corresponds to me..." I took everything with ambition and went far from his presence to use it all up and waste my life. Again, I prepared my suitcases to, in my opinion, "fly higher."

I told him I would go far away, where I could hide from his presence. But how ignorant I am! I never thought there was no place where I could hide from his presence, where he would not be watching me! Because it is true, he is everywhere, everything is his, and he encompasses everything.

"Where can I go from Your Spirit? Where can I flee from Your presence? If I ascend to heaven, You are there; if I make my bed in the sun, You are there. If I take the wings of the morning and dwell in the farthest parts of the sea, even there, Your hand will lead me, and Your right hand will hold me. If I say, 'Surely the darkness will cover me,' even the night will shine around me. 'Even the darkness will not cover me from You, and the night shines like the day; darkness and light are both Yours. ' For You formed my inward parts and made me in my mother's womb." Psalm 139:7-13 (NKJV)

Now I can say it: that spiritual inheritance that I asked for at a very early stage of my life, I did not deserve it. I stole it like a thief and ran away. I snatched it from him and went far away from him. It seemed that I had forgotten that there was still a God who was watching me, that same God who had taken me from my land to bring me to faraway places so that I could reach Him, that God with the power to make rivers of living water flow for my life and for your life, and that water quenches our spiritual thirst and becomes blessings for our lives. But I left without his permission and walked away with the inheritance, not because I deserved it, but because of my stubbornness and disobedience.

**Now I understand that God always lets you go through circumstances in your life that help you understand that another call is coming, an incredible calling. I believe that at that time, I had discovered many things and been dazzled by many situations, but I was not prepared for what He wanted to do with me.**

My rebellion did not allow Him to use me as a clay vessel to mold me into His form. It is not that He did not have the power to do so. Still, He needed to allow me to return to that life entirely of doubts, questions, and confusion, to that great emptiness that I always had so that I could hit rock bottom a little more, and so He could express His glory over me, and all for His honor.

At that time, I never heard His voice telling me: "Don't leave my House," but now I think that He told me: "If you want to leave, there is the door," just like a mother or father says to their children when they want to leave Home before their time before they are adults. "Do you want to leave? Come on, go ahead; you will have to learn about life as it is, far from the protection of the mother or the father." Leaving like that, sad and without hope, because there is no place for our soul to rest.

Who would have thought that when I began to pack my belongings, they were only pride, greed, vanity, resentment, anger, and my

## 4. WHEN EARTHLY RICHES DO NOT FILL THE HEART

human ambitions, which weighed too much in my suitcase; as best I could, I headed towards a new path to show everything I could achieve with my "wisdom and my power," thinking that everything had started wonderfully. When the truth is that it was not like that; without knowing it, I was entering a new place that was unknown in my life. I was in the land of Egypt, thinking that this was the promised land.

I was lost, taking false steps, because I had no guidance to get in the right direction to give me the best life success. In Egypt, I did not find rest for my soul; there, I faced anguish, misery, and sorrow. I was very far from the Promised Land, from the meaning of the Promised Land, which is a place of peace and total rest, and that place of tranquility is Jesus Christ himself. But my path took another direction, and I strayed too far.

As time passed, I faced the consequences. Now I can say that, whether you decide to embark on any journey and in any direction, you must consider who will be accompanying you, you must be alert to who will approach you as a guide on your path. I made the mistake of straying from the path I was on; I left because it was too easy for me to lead that life "as a new creature in Christ," I did not value it, and I thought it was a minimal existence, too simple and not very exciting, besides, on that divine path I did not find many traces of those who had traveled that path; because that path is narrow and what I needed was a map of masses who had already traveled that path.

Now I know that this path is very exclusive, very VIP-style, and not many can walk it because it is challenging, although, in the end, it has a prize so grand that it cannot be compared to any wealth or all the gold in the world, and the reward is the salvation of the soul.

I was only looking for a "better" place, but on the earthly plane, and in that search, I was losing the most essential plane, the true one that offers you eternal life.

The path of salvation seemed very complex and too narrow to me, I could not look well to the sides or in front: now I understand, I was wrong. I thought it was not the right path because it was too narrow. After all, I could not see well what was around me, so I opted for the broad path because it was pretty open, and there were masses of people who walked it; on that broad path, I believed that I could find many more options to live, there was no need to overthink or make too many efforts because there were already billions who saw a certain way, they had a lot of freedom in their way of living, of speaking and without any fear.

When I embarked on that path so well known to the world and not to those who chose the narrow path, I began to experience a very easy-to-follow lifestyle. There was no one to tell you whether this was right or not. Everything was like "YOLO": "you only live once", you only live once, so you had to enjoy it to the fullest "like there is no tomorrow", as if there were no tomorrow.

At that time, I thought that if everything was going wonderfully, it was because of God's will because He did not want me to suffer or have restrictions in my life. I thought, "He wants me to have a happy and full life, full of abundance," but what I never felt and did not have discernment at that time was that the deceptions of the enemy enter your life in this way, everything seems very good and even with a life entire of prosperity to suddenly catch you and take possession of your existence. That is why I told you not to be deceived.

## 4. WHEN EARTHLY RICHES DO NOT FILL THE HEART

**The enemy comes into your life disguised so that you feel tempted to discover him, so that you do not run away from him and, on the contrary, accept him and open the doors of your life to him. You must know that a true enemy does not enter your life with a sword and make war on you, no. He enters very kindly and speaks to you with sweet words and even with gifts, his purpose is to seduce you, envelop you, and trap you, so you must be careful, perhaps what I am telling you can help you unmask that enemy who wants to destroy your life with material things and pleasures, he wants to take away your eternal joy by giving you many temporary things and pleasures. This happened to me.**

I thought my life was going great; I felt I had everything I had always wanted since childhood; everything I had always dreamed of and longed for was coming true. I thought I lacked nothing, that God had wonderfully blessed me beyond any words I could express. I felt I achieved everything quickly: everything I set out to do and everything I longed for. In those days, I thought I was capable of anything and that anything I undertook would succeed.

I must tell you that one of my goals was to be an entrepreneur. I remember that from a very young age I have had a strong entrepreneurial spirit, a leader, a great desire to communicate with people. I like business and sales, and I have always wanted to measure and challenge human potential to exceed expectations in sales. I was not afraid of anything, and I was the first to take it on if there was a challenge. I believed I could achieve everything, overcome any adversity, be better and more confident, bolder and more daring every day.

But how ironic to tell you this: I was afraid of the essential thing in my life, and I ran away from it like a coward, even though it was "the best business in the world," the one that was going to give me the best profits, more than any investment or business I had ever made in my entire life. All I needed to obtain the maximum profit was to be faithful because, in the end, He has the grand prize prepared for those who open their doors to Him and are loyal. The award is enormous, very prestigious, and has the best designation that surpasses many others in the world. It is a prize without monetary value, which is not won at any price.

Today, I remind you that if you already live these moments, do not let them go. Do not allow anyone to take them away because many will try to take you from where God wants to put you. And if you are not yet on the way to the Lord's Home, look for Him so that no one can take possession of that blessing that belongs only to you. Return Home.

How can I forget that first business I had? It was a high-yield venture, knocking on doors and selling a product in various places in California. I am not ashamed to say this because I want it to motivate many people who wish to undertake to start an adventure. It is challenging, and we never know if it will be a success or a total failure. However, the decision will lead us to take the risk and think about the complications; we will have to learn to put professional and personal priorities in their proper place.

I was 23 years old at that time and I knocked on doors and doors without any fear, I was willing to sacrifice, to talk to strangers and if someone rejected my offers it did not bother me at all, my mo-

## 4. WHEN EARTHLY RICHES DO NOT FILL THE HEART

rale did not drop, on the contrary! I told myself: "You can do it!" If potential clients told me "no," I asked them, "Who do you know that you can recommend to me and who might be interested in my product." What I wanted was to expand my business because I dreamed big, my expectations had no limits and, without being conceited, I must say that every step I took forward, a step that led to professional success.

I will tell you about an experience I will never forget, an event that left a deep mark on me in those days. As I told you, I had given my life to God and had been baptized. My mother had also given her life to the Lord and remained faithful. I made great efforts during those years to achieve a better economic position and was full of strength and confidence. I worked with great enthusiasm. One of my first checks for my commissions in my first business as an entrepreneur, for that time and my age, was for a perfect amount of money, a large amount, especially for a young woman like me.

I remember having the check in my hands, and with great emotion, full of happiness, I showed it to my mother and said: "Look, Mom, this check that they gave me!" She looked at the check I had in my hands, then looked up and stared at me with a solemn and sad expression, then she said to me: "My daughter, do not let money change your way of thinking and being," and her eyes filled with tears that she began to wipe away with her tired hands.

My mother raised me with great sacrifice. She was referring to the fact that I had moved away from the house of God and that now, with so much money in my hands, I would completely forget about that first love and would have more love for money, for the things of the world, for greed, and that would lead me to perdition, to forgetting definitively where I came from without wanting to look back, without remembering the promise I had made to the Lord, forgetting my humility, my trust in God.

When I looked at my sad mother, seeing her tears in that expression of pain, I just remained silent, put the check in my bag, and left. Those words from my mother marked me forever, after that occasion I thought very often about her words, they were like a reminder that always came to me warning me what were the significant things and what we had to value.

**And if I ever got lost, forgot my origins, or denied who I was, my people, my childhood, my roots, even if I did not return to the house of God, I knew that, no matter how many my falls and failures to his loyalty were, even if I was very far from the house of God, He would always be there, with me.**

All my life, I have felt a lot of love for my family. I love my roots and always try to share them with my family, no matter my life level. My mother, with her words and her example, taught me to remember that I must be humble, but at that time, I lived in great confusion. I believed that being "good" was enough to be right with God, that even if I only gave Him those crumbs of love, He would be satisfied with me. He does not need crumbs of love or of being a good Samaritan, He asks for something more than that; He wants us to give Him our life and be faithful to Him. I must confess that I was away from the house of God for 22 years. What an eternity and what a waste of time, almost a lifetime! But He is always faithful, shows His love, and is never late. After all those years that I abandoned Him,

## 4. WHEN EARTHLY RICHES DO NOT FILL THE HEART

God did something supernatural in my life so that I could kneel at His feet. He showed me with His light and power that His way back Home awaited me.

I distanced myself from His presence and His grace. I thought that just "believing in Him" was enough. I did not know about His mercy because I was focused on earthly gifts, on companies that gave me money, some luxuries, and comforts.

My time was focused on working and making money, showing that I was not afraid of becoming a leading businesswoman. Everything that made me great had to do with material things, the power of money, business, and pride.

I let myself be carried away by my ego and did not think about God with a genuine conscience. I believed that only thanking Him superficially would cover my poor quota of faith, but happiness was only momentary; successes lasted minimally and sometimes plunged me into anguish, worries, physical pain, and a strange emptiness that at that moment was not filled with anything, not with trips or with the purchase of valuable things.

Later, I understood that I lived with a huge emotional void; only a tiny part of me was fulfilled by business, tireless work, and the acquisition of objects for a comfortable and superficial life. Until God showed me a path I had already traveled, but because of my pride I pushed aside; then God showed me a new covenant and the opportunity to recognize what I had lost, God wanted me back Home so that He could work great miracles in my life.

5

# 5
# Walking towards the light

I always liked to work on my personal development and have very high expectations for my life. I think I was even quite strict with myself. If I had to work, I had to put in my maximum effort.

I was tireless. I signed up for every self-improvement course I could find or motivational workshop. I was always —and I have been looking for it for as long as I can remember— looking for ways to improve and feel better, more complete, and constantly challenging myself.

I have liked to read for years, so I bought books all the time and spent every morning reading works on various subjects, except those that had to do with the word of God. Ever since I can remember, I have been a very restless person.

Despite my great rebellion with God, I have always felt that in anything I set out to do, there is a force behind me that drives me and helps me achieve all my goals, but what I did not know was that God was lighting my way, He was my shepherd so that I would not stray too far from His flock because He had a better plan for me, an admirable light, at the same time He confirmed to me that there is nothing wrong with having ambitions in life, trying to achieve specific goals and wanting to improve ourselves. God's great purpose is to make us return Home to the place where God transforms our pain into purpose.

**God can help us achieve what we want. It is not a sin to aspire to live better, to enjoy a triumph that gives us a better way of living. The problem lies in establishing priorities in your life and where you put God. Is he on your list of priorities or at the end of your list with the daily things you plan to do?**

We must be careful not to reach a point in life where we think we have everything but feel like we have nothing. Reach a point where you are working tirelessly to have something and achieve your goals, and realize that you worked tirelessly for the wrong things. In the end, you will feel like you are in spiritual ruin, in a dark abyss where all the effort was in vain. I will tell you about this.

I want to share with you some reflections that have to do with valuing and knowing how to pay attention to the messages of others. For this, I must say that one of the greatest passions I have had is not only telling stories to others but also listening to stories from others, from family members and people close to me, and those who know me know this very well. I am passionate about sitting down to listen to stories about outstanding achievements or stories of defeats, challenges, or great tragedies that human beings experience.

I loved hearing how there were people who managed to rise from the most significant problems and complications, from accidents or internal conflicts, or knowing about other beings who were

## 5. WALKING TOWARDS THE LIGHT

still sunk in their tragedies, trapped in their problems, whom I saw with tremendous despair on their shoulders because they could not find a way out of their sorrows or something that could free them from all their bonds. Now I understand it and know that deep within me, I understood the answers to those stories. I learned how all of them could be transformed into victories.

Without a doubt, you who are reading me have gone through many moments of light and shadow, perhaps great joys or enormous sadness; only you know how many bad experiences, failures, defeats, and disappointments you have lived, to the point of feeling that your strength is running out, and you cannot go on. I understand you; sometimes, we believe that we will not be able to find the solution to our problems.

There even comes a point where the tiredness is so great and overwhelming that instead of thinking about what you are going through, you try to ignore the difficult situations you are going through and walk through life aimlessly, without finding any meaning in existence. Without hope, you go with the flow, further and further away from relief and closer to pain, because there comes a time in life when the burden we carry is too heavy to continue, and then we stop finding meaning in life.

If, on the other hand, you have had a "happy" life, full of luxuries and without financial problems, you have everything you always wanted, you had a happy childhood, and you have formed a family marked by happiness, if you had a perfect family and school education that led you to achieve beautiful goals, good job positions, or you have consolidated very successful businesses of your own.

In both cases, I would like to sit down with you, get to know you, and listen to your testimony because your story is worth a lot, no matter if it is one of success or defeat, no matter the challenges you have gone through and what you have lived, you should know that you are not alone because your life has a greater calling or a purpose greater than what your eyes can see.

I confess this to you because I spent almost my entire life as if I were alone in the world, in this complex world revolving around me while my brain was racing in all directions without any certainty, always seeking to find a solution for everything and everyone.

**I am clear that I was lost and alone, even though surrounded by people. It is true that leaving the gospel, the house of God, made me feel more lost, confused, and abandoned, even more than those who have never known the gospel.**

If you have had the opportunity to be in the house of the Lord, and that seed was planted in your heart, and then you abandoned everything, be very careful because that can be a delicate point in your life. After all, although you may appreciate the blessings of God far from Him and believe that you are doing His will, God can give you those earthly fruits so that you can enjoy them temporarily. Still, He does not want us to experience only small things; He wants us to look at "The Big Picture," that enormous, eternal panorama, and take possession of His reward, those of us who are faithful to Him full-time.

There are those who say that God is a God of love. Indeed, He is. But He is also a God who greatly values your loyalty and humility; it hurts Him when we fail and disobey Him. What happened to King Nebuchadnezzar in the book of Daniel? He became filled with pride

## 5. WALKING TOWARDS THE LIGHT

and stubbornness; all his power was taken away from him, and his glory was gone. The great lesson of that story is that we must always be humble and obey God's laws. His plans never fail. Every period of difficulty, even suffering, has its end and its lesson.

Those who have never experienced the proper knowledge of the gospel or no one has shown them its greatness cannot understand what it means to be at Home or not to be. Still, for those of us who were there one day and decided to leave, we understand the significant weight it brings to our lives.

The enemy who is in the world surrounds us with the things that are in the world and, as I said, puts a big blindfold on our eyes so doesn't look and entangles us with multiple visions that prevent our brain from thinking well and acting under the will of God, looking back at what we left behind and what we are missing, a life of joy with great hopes, more significant than any tribulation you are going through in your current life.

That is why I invite you to stay here, with these words intended to share a story of falls, defeats, and light, a story of what I did to return Home. These lines that I wrote are for you; what I am telling you has nothing to do with whether you have a high or low social position, whether you have a lot of money or lack it, nor if you are a person with a very high education, or you never went to school. I am about to confess something very special to me, and I want to be honest with you and tell you something before continuing. I will reveal to you that I do not do it to feel like a particular person or boast. Furthermore, I do not pretend to give myself any credit or believe myself better than anyone because I am clear: I am ignorant before the presence of God, but I confess to you that there is a supernatural power that can come into your life at any moment and this fundamental moment is to bless you, never to destroy you.

I have always felt that we should look for something more. From a young age, I perceived something was wrong with what I saw and felt. I often found myself sad, alone and with a great emptiness in my life. All of this was turning into a lot of bitterness, rebellion, and too much anger. That's right, everything made me angry. Despite so many things I achieved in my life, I felt that something was still missing, and this unpleasant feeling made me feel lost as I navigated life outside of Home. That rebellion, with its pride, had me blinded, stubborn in my anger, and without appreciating what had come for good in my life—that I myself had let it slip through my hands!

I had already forgotten my first love, that House where I had been and where I felt safe, that House that I abandoned and that kept me spiritually far away. Yes, I felt lost, away from Home. I thought I had everything, but at the same time, I felt like I had nothing; I was only the owner of a constant emotional exhaustion that overwhelmed me for a long time.

I thought I had much to offer others, but I could not share anything with just one person. So I walked through the world, seemingly aware of the places I was heading, but it seemed like only an invisible force was guiding me, and in the end, I asked myself: "How did I get here and for what?" Because what I was always looking for was something more, something to fill that great emptiness I felt. I also had a permanent feeling of loneliness, the sense that there must

## 5. WALKING TOWARDS THE LIGHT

be something more powerful somewhere, something bigger than my past that could be like a giant stone to climb and offer its secrets.

If I tell you that I felt lost, it is because I lived in a state of absolute despair, as if I were trapped in a dark place, a dark, bleak valley full of darkness where I could not see well, even what was closest.

That is how I felt. In a place where you cannot perceive what is closest to you, where you cannot take a safe step to know the direction in which you are going and much less look back or where you come from, and everything was useless because looking in any direction made me think that I had already walked a lot in the darkness. If I looked back, I felt that I could stay there, stagnant, until I lost my life, without any chance of knowing what I could do later to get out of there.

That is how I spent my days. Emotionally and spiritually lost, people spoke to me, and I did not pay attention; my mind was somewhere else, my body was present, but my feelings were somewhere else. Time passed, and the feeling of being lost increased every day. Very quickly it was as if the clock was turning quickly, and time was running out, running out so that I could not achieve what I was called to do.

I reached a point of feeling emotionally and physically exhausted; my mind and body were spinning from one side to the other without finding peace anywhere. I was constantly adjusting situations or emotions that I felt were not balanced. I was fixing everything that was no longer working, but even though I intended to do that, it turned out that I was fixing something, and the rest was improper.

In the end, when everything was apparently in its place, I would break it all up again to start putting everything in order again. I did this all the time, doing and undoing, and it was very exhausting. I lived with the feeling that something would come. I thought that something would happen, and I had to prepare myself. So the years went by...

I went through many valleys of insecurity. Yes, with a life of many achievements, but also numerous disappointments, sadness, constant anguish, a tremendous feeling of insecurity, and no fixed direction to go. I felt like I was walking through a place that was too wide, so vast that I thought that the more time passed, the wider it became, and the feeling of being lost and confused grew even more on that path.

We must be cautious when walking that wide path because we will find too many deceptive options there. Currently, it is believed that if we have many options to do things, it is perfect, but be very careful because the more options there are, the more we will reach a moment when we will come across a wall, and we will not know whether to jump over it, go left, right or go back. However, walking along a narrow path, we must advance diligently and fulfill our fruitful purposes.

Although I know that the people who knew me saw me as an empowered, talented, self-confident, and successful woman, what the world didn't know, nor did I, was that I was living a great war inside me, a terrible battle with myself and with everything around me. A bomb was inside me, about to explode.

This is how I lived a large part of my life and, unfortunately, this is how millions of human beings live in these times: a life without a fixed direction and without a clear idea of why we came to this world

## 5. WALKING TOWARDS THE LIGHT

and for what, a life of emptiness, confusion, loneliness... This is how I lived. For a long time, I thought I would find the truth to so many doubts, the answers to so many questions, to discover the reasons for all those emotions derived from an existence entirely of turmoil.

Externally, it might seem that I was living a fulfilled life, financially, professionally, and personally, a happy life, but I was deeply unhappy with myself and with others; ignorant, I thought that there was another better way to live and that I would find all the answers, so I began to walk down that very long and wide path, I started to read books in search of help, to listen to audios and participate in personal development seminars and even courses on how to heal your inner child.

I was busy searching for total success in all areas of my life, trying to fill that void and find what I believed was my purpose in life.

I wanted to turn that rebellion and all those frustrations into happiness under my understanding and wisdom. Thus, every day that passed, I not only spent much more money on all those courses that I bought, but that only brought more confusion to my life, causing a tremendous emotional disorder that I also had to face.

I didn't understand what was happening to me. I was overcome by a feeling of enormous desolation, an isolation from myself, from where I belonged. I don't know if you've felt this. It's like when you leave Home for a trip and arrive at another Home or hotel room. Maybe the first few days, you feel happy and content, but as the days go by, little by little, you start to feel uncomfortable, agitated, and tired because you want to go back Home because your Home brings you peace, and you feel comfortable in your own space.

## RETURN HOME

That's how I felt, and it wasn't for a short time like when we go on a short trip. My trip was very long, a trip that should have been my permanent Home because I lived there for many years, and I never felt safe. I never had a feeling of clarity or certainty, at least what I thought was safety or balance. According to my expectations, it wasn't the right path to follow.

I continued in the search to reach a place where I could have a "better life." The years went by, and every day, I felt worse, more confused, and with a mind that felt more and more numb than the day before, more entangled, and with less understanding of where I was situated in life.

I escaped loneliness, but I felt overwhelmed in the middle of so many people; I didn't fit in anywhere, I felt like I didn't belong to any group of people, that if I opened my mouth to express myself no one would listen to me or understand me, I was sunk in a feeling of isolation, distrust, and insurmountable emptiness. Time went by, and I felt lost more and more. Even though I apparently had everything I had longed for financially, that I didn't have any illnesses, and I always felt loved by my family, I still endured the tremendous emptiness of my life, and there was nothing that could fill it.

I remember that some girls once commented to me about how they felt about life, their concerns, and their needs. They told me that if they had the financial means I had, they would buy many things they had wanted for a long time and would even get some plastic surgery. I just kept quiet, thinking about their desires, "Why do I want that? Why change how I am, how I look? Why buy the things they want? What I need is to get out of this desert I find myself in and

## 5. WALKING TOWARDS THE LIGHT

discover my path," because all that emptiness that surrounded me was turning into a feeling of anger and bitterness. It is like when deep in our hearts we know that we are not where we want to be, we are not performing as spiritually as we should.

Because we must remember that by nature, we are spiritual creatures, and at some point in our lives, we must understand that we are falling short of doing what is God's will. And maybe you ask yourself: How do I know if I am doing God's will? How do I know things are oriented to His will and not under my will? Why is it that sometimes, even if you do everything possible to achieve something, your effort is insufficient, things do not turn out the way you wanted, and you do not feel satisfied with what you accomplished? Because we do not focus or are consistent in what is demanded of us as believers. One day, we start one thing, then we get angry and do something else.

Have you ever wondered what the purpose of your life is? And, if you have gone through many ups and downs of feelings and confusion, you ask yourself what else is there for me in this life? And that is why you seek to fill your emptiness or simply the curiosity awakens in you to know if there is something in the life of a human being that cannot be seen, something much more significant that there is still no person with the highest intelligence and outstanding wisdom who can grasp and from which you can benefit, I insist, something that cannot be seen, but exists, yes. It is for you, and it is within your reach.

I must clarify that I am sharing everything I have been through with you because I would like it to help you answer some of your concerns. I would like everything I have had to go through to help you find your way and understand the "reason why" of everything you have been through so that you can make a good decision and choose the right path in times of great uncertainty.

After years of darkness, I now understand many things, including that the path I have walked my whole life was extensive and is the same path that almost all of humanity is currently walking. We are in an era where we want everything straightforward and fast, so we take the wide path. However, how do we know if the path I am crossing is wide? How do we know if we will find the solution to this permanent search to understand what we are and why we are here?

Let me ask you more questions: Is your life very similar to that of your friends? Are your daily activities, the way you dress, the type of music you listen to, the places you frequent, the way you think, and even the way you use vocabulary similar? Is that how you lead your life? Do you spend your life imitating what most people around you do, not only in the circle of people you know but even in the world, in what you see on social media and television?

That is why I invite you to get out of that vicious circle. Do not be afraid to look at yourself or be different from others. Do not fear being told that you are strange and look very different in these worldly times and in this society. Because this world is not our eternal Home, we are just passing through. We have an eternal Home waiting for us with a great welcome, and everything will be in its time, in the place that God has assigned to us.

That was my life. And unfortunately, that is also the life of most people.

I think I have lived long enough to realize that I was not the only person who had a lost life and was far from finding the way back Home.

## 5. WALKING TOWARDS THE LIGHT

In those years I found myself in the desert, lost in that wasteland and in the darkest night, surrounded by a terrible loneliness, I thought I was the only one, the most miserable and alone being. Today, I know that this is not the case because afterward, I was frequently approached by women asking me for advice on what to do with their professional lives and even with their personal lives, women who perhaps experienced the same loneliness and spiritual misery as I did.

I seemed very confident and had the appearance of someone who knew the right direction to direct his life. So, I listened to all those women who came to me with a great desire to help them find the path to a better life. I sat down and listened to them with great attention. I truly felt a great desire to help them because, in a certain way, they were reflections of my own anxieties and frustrations.

Now I think that deep in my heart, it was always a great passion in my life to find the truth; I always felt that it was a duty, an obligation to leave the desert in which I was lost and open the way for a new generation. That is why what I saw and heard from the people who approached me to tell me their experiences brought me even more pressure to not only find the path so necessary for me, I knew that I was deeply lost like those women who approached me to tell me their concerns, and that reinforced my desire to discover the path that would take me back Home and feel safe again.

I remember that on one occasion, a woman who had also left her town in Mexico when she was twelve and very young came to me. She was from Durango and told me that tragedies and violence marked her family life, that there were not many displays of love between her parents and siblings, and that this tortured her a lot.

She told me that her grandfather kidnapped a young woman he later made his wife when she was fifteen years old. He was almost twenty years older than her and gave her a miserable life. He beat her if she didn't do things the way he wanted to be done; he humiliated her, and even though she later asked for forgiveness, the damage was done. Things got worse when the man got drunk, demanded money, food, and alcohol, and mistreated her for anything. However, she remained silent, she must, because the times she tried to defend herself, her husband's demands increased.

Her poor children saw with horror the violent way in which their father acted, and the next day, more with fear than with genuine affection, they hugged him and kissed him so that he would no longer get angry with them and would not hit their mother. The children, without knowing it, received all the emotional burden of that life of blows, insults, and violence; the father hugged them and told them that he loved them very much; he tried to speak well to their mother, and although some days it seemed that everything would be fine, things were altered and broken by any disagreement, even if it was small.

This woman also told me that one day, she discovered that her grandfather had grown up an orphan. From a very young age, he had taken care of his younger siblings, and although he had a father, he always treated him rudely, humiliated him, and hit him to make him "become a man." He would scold him if he didn't do the things he had asked him to do properly. He would hit him with a belt if he lost money or forgot his orders, so his life was hell.

The woman also told me that her mother, who remembered very well the beatings, mistreatment, and abuse she received from her

## 5. WALKING TOWARDS THE LIGHT

father, that is, her grandfather, when he grew old, stayed to live in her house with her daughter. However, although he sometimes asked for forgiveness, if for some reason he drank alcohol at a birthday party, he behaved stubbornly. He reminded the mother of all the suffering they had gone through with his words and actions.

When she told me this, the woman cried for her mother, even for her grandfather and for her family, because she, she confessed to me, was like her grandfather: she did not feel attached to her children, she did not love her brothers as she said she should love them, and she felt very angry with people who looked well and happy. In short, she confessed to me crying; she had no desire to live, she was angry about her life, and she felt that God was never there for her.

I listened to her and kept thinking about how many women like her, and thousands of men, too, have gone through stories like this. How many men and women have we seen or suffered from lack of love, deception, or cruelty? How many women and men have been rude or have hurt someone? How many times have we been so lost, with so much pain, hate, and resentment, so empty and alone, so far from having a genuine relationship with God? As I said, just like when you are young, and you hear that God created us, but we do not feel that tenderness on his part, his company on our path, and we can even less know where we are going with our heavy load, this does not indicate that He does not have a love for us.

That is why my reason for living now is to help with all my experience, passion, and, above all, with all my humility, without ego or pride, so that, together, we rise from our defeats to other dimensions where God wants us to find ourselves.

**Now I know that the ideal in life is to always look for a way to find clarity, to be like those eagles that, despite suffering, anguish, and the most relentless storms, seek to overcome adversity with unwavering faith and rise to those dimensions where everything will be fine.**

I would very much like my life testimony to serve to help people and to tell them that I understand their tribulations and troubles because I, too, was a woman who went astray and suffered a lot of pain, and unfortunately, that is how most people live today. But yes, it is possible to come out of the darkness towards the magnificent Light of God; yes, we can break every chain of bondage in our lives if we accept to enter the narrow path, which is precisely the path that takes us back Home and keeps us in that peace.

# 6

# Paths through distant lands

Although God places us in special circumstances for a unique purpose, we must be prepared to experience loneliness and despair while navigating these unfamiliar paths. The truth is that at the end of that journey, light will emerge.

Years went by, and I began to realize that everything I had done throughout my life was merely preparation for what I was experiencing at that moment: a life centered on earthly achievements based on societal expectations.

Throughout our lives, from childhood to adulthood, we are taught certain things deemed necessary for fulfillment. These beliefs emphasize what is valued and socially acceptable, such as education, material possessions, the neighborhood we reside in, the type of car we drive, the brand of clothing we wear, how often we vacation, and, most importantly, our financial achievements accumulated in the shortest time possible.

In today's society, youth are often judged based on milestones like purchasing a Home at an early age, having investments, and maintaining a substantial savings account. These accomplishments are frequently deemed indicators of great success.

**However, success is not measured by how much money you have in your savings account or whether you own property, a new model car, or a business that makes millions of dollars. Here, it is appropriate to ask, but how good is your relationship with God? Or how much do you obey Him?**

So, is it true that if you are doing so well in these material aspects, you are also doing well with God because you are achieving your full potential here on earth? You have not failed God by being successful because you have not had a mediocre life. We know that there is nothing wrong with receiving a good education in a high-level school, driving a good car, or dressing very well, but what is worth asking is if we know how to arrange the priorities in our life, if we are capable of choosing the most important things for us and if God is in that selection of the most relevant.

This is precisely what happened to me. I let myself slip into the same current that drags the world, the majority of people, doing things that gave me economic wealth but were not spiritually necessary; I followed a path without a fixed destination, and the current took me without knowing where. And what happens when you don't have a fixed direction, anywhere to go, a fixed goal to accomplish, or an eternal Home at the end of your journey? Well, what happens is that suddenly, you find yourself walking in the desert, lost, with great emptiness, and alone, without seeing the way out to get to the place that God wanted for you.

When we do not allow God to work in our lives and take us where He wants us to be under His purpose and not under our

## 6. PATHS THROUGH DISTANT LANDS

ephemeral desires, the enemy takes possession of the path and takes us through dark places and dry, dark, frozen lands. Remember: "Do not store up for yourselves treasures on earth, where moth and rust destroy, and where thieves break in and steal. For where your treasure is, there your heart will be also." Matthew 6:19-34 (NKJV). What wonderful words! They are a sign of a promise that we must always keep in mind to discard thoughts that make us work very hard, only to value earthly efforts and not divine wealth. That is why I ask: How much credit do you have with Him?

Where are you putting your mind and your priorities? If we accept His call, we will be able to live our whole lives, as day after day, God reveals to us more and more of the purpose He has prepared for us since before the foundation of the world. I confess I had zero credit with Him. Instead, I had a huge debt to Him, and even if I spent the rest of my life accumulating billions of dollars, I would never be able to pay that debt. I had abandoned Him and I snatched away His inheritance, yes, I stole it from Him without deserving it! There was only one way I could pay that debt, and I will tell you how I spent it. And when you pay that debt, even with some extra and some interest, He will set you free from all ties.

First, I want to tell you how, for a while, I felt totally disturbed and overwhelmed by my life. Around 2008, I began to feel a hunger and thirst to know more, to know more about human potential, and at the same time, I had a great desire to see how far my potential could go.

With these thoughts in mind, filled with ambitions and establishing categories of value, the only thing sure was that I was hopelessly lost because I had forgotten who had given me everything! I had nothing, absolutely nothing. I was broke, and my thoughts were only dark and dry. But one day, God mercifully gave me more than I could have imagined. Despite the gifts He had given me, it turns out that I was trying to understand more about human power, and out of ignorance, perhaps pride, I felt that only I had the power and wisdom to do things and create an extraordinary life. To my surprise and better "luck," He had a better plan for my life; He would take me to other levels that He had prepared for me. It is an excellent plan I would never have thought existed, not even in the most beautiful story I have ever read.

At that time, something unknown and severe was happening in my life. I felt a great disturbance that stopped all my purposes of moving forward. I was reaching a point where something was no longer working well. For example, when your vehicle has a problem with the engine or some other part, it prevents you from moving forward. That was how I struggled to keep moving forward, trying changes and planning things that were not done. I was reaching a point where everything I did seemed to have no life. An incredible force behind all this prevented things from being carried out. At that moment, I could feel that everything was dying in me, and I was living in a desert, in a dry, desolate land, where no fruit or flower was reborn, and I felt all this very strongly to the depths of my heart.

I didn't know that He would come to that dry land to speak to me, touch my heart, rescue me, and accommodate me in a perfect place chosen for my life. He allowed me to go through the lowest things so that later, they would manifest beautifully in my life, and I

## 6. PATHS THROUGH DISTANT LANDS

would be a testimony to His people. Please listen to me carefully: if you are going through difficult times right now and feel that you cannot find a way out of the trap, I ask you to pay attention, do not try to go back in time, and ask yourself, "Why me?" Do not try to find a way out without knowing why God put you there. If you leave without reflecting on it, you may get away a little from the complicated situation you are in, but then you will return to it because that is not His will, and then you will find yourself in a vicious circle.

God is in the disturbance of your destiny, allowing you to reflect on your actions to put yourself in His perfect plan. So in that state of desolation in which you find yourself, open your mouth, speak, raise your voice, and ask Him not to take you out of there until you know exactly where He wants you to go; tell Him not to take you where you want to go, but where He wants to take you, only then will your path be prosperous and everything will turn out well.

That year, when I began the deep search to know and understand more about the emptiness I felt and that I could not fill with something to relieve my restlessness, I also had in the depths of my heart a feeling that what was happening had nothing to do with His call, as I said, something did not fit in my life. I had everything, but at the same time, I had nothing; I only felt that deep emptiness where there was nothing, occasion, or person that could help me fill it; I felt hollow, dry, with an enormous lack of vision of my own identity, trapped in a devastating feeling that turned into anger, bitterness, miserable life and even a sense of madness.

I was in spiritual ruin: I was nothing, and I could give nothing. And how strange, even though I never experienced limitations in anything, thank God. I have already said that I have always been a woman who likes to get ahead in all areas of life. Still, at that time, spiritually, I did not have that "performance" nor the answers that my soul longed for, and, worst of all, it was too late to stop the life that was taking me directly to the desert, or instead I had already been in the desert for several years. I had not realized that darkness arose with greater force where I was, and the possibility that something powerful could manifest was very remote.

How ironic to think now about the path that led me back Home because before I found Him, I used to get physically lost on the roads I walked on, or instead, the Almighty led me along long paths in the desert until I was on my knees before His presence. Now, I have had a lot of time to think about everything that happened over the years, and I ask myself: "Hilda, why did it take you so long to realize what was happening to you without noticing that God was speaking to you so clearly?" But it was true. I hadn't seen it then; before I knew it, I had already been walking in the desert. I remember the first time I was in Iran, in Tehran, around 2005.

I think I have been living there for four months. One day, around nine in the morning and feeling very alone and sad, missing my family, my Home, and my city, suddenly I said to myself, "This day I am going to disappear; I don't care if I get lost and don't find my way back, whatever God wants." Without telling anyone, I dressed adequately, covered my head, had my hijab intact, and put some money in it.

My phone was in the pocket of a long coat I had (remember that I was in an Islamic country, so I had to be very well covered and

## 6. PATHS THROUGH DISTANT LANDS

my coat covered my whole body, as for my head, there was not a single hair sticking out). I should not draw attention to myself because the police could even take me away if I broke their rules.

That morning was the first time I walked alone through the streets without knowing how to go. I just wanted to experience walking alone, without any known presence at my side. I know it sounds strange, but that's really how it was, just walking, getting lost in those streets of that unknown city, and seeing if I could have the ability or intelligence to return Home without anyone's help.

Tehran is the capital of Iran, with a population of approximately nine or ten million people. As you can imagine, it is a very populated place with small, narrow streets saturated with cars, people, and shops, where many motorcyclists run through the pedestrian zones, get on the sidewalks, and advance at high speed between the vehicles as if they didn't care about running someone over. With so much movement of cars and people, the streets are a total disaster: that was my spiritual life. And there I was. A Mexican woman who, during my first year in Iran, did not speak Farsi, although that did not prevent me from crossing the streets where I could not stop hearing the sound of car horns everywhere, the voices of people, and the noise of the big city; who would have said that such a daring experience would serve as a parable to tell them that later I would find myself in the middle of the desert, that a supernatural force would arrive to snatch me from that place and show me the way back Home.

That day in the streets of Tehran, I was aware that one more step I took could mean a greater distance from the path of return, but that was not a difficulty for me. I was willing to get lost and experience what it felt like to travel there. I knew that in the next attempt, I would succeed in finding the way back Home.

I remember that on that long walk, I stopped several times to look at the enormous buildings. Furthermore, I was amazed by the signs I found on the streets, the shops, the warehouses, the illuminated advertisements, and the posters; there were walls impregnated by smoke and old buildings that seemed to belong to a story of ancient stories, at one point I decided to sit in a small café. I ordered a cup of that rich drink with a delicious cake, and while I enjoyed it alone, I contemplated the rhythm of the streets, the cars, the people, the children, and the sky clouded by pollution.

You may be wondering, but what does this story have to do with being lost in the desert? And the answer is everything. Analyze carefully what I tell you, not only about this part of my story but yours.

There are times when you are looking for some way to find a way out of your complications, solutions to fill some emptiness, or some answer to get out of Home, a way of life, out of your world that overwhelms you. Then you try to take a step forward without really knowing what awaits you because maybe in that attempt you will get more lost, you will get doubly confused, or you may find the truth that you have been seeking with so much effort, the solution to your problems. And if you realize that is how we get along, like lost in streets, labyrinths, noises, shop windows, looking for the answer to something that you will not find in that confusion, on the contrary, you will get more lost.

You will have more questions and concerns because the answer will be given only when you are at Home or turn to it where you belong. Then you will prosper, and everything will turn out well for you.

## 6. PATHS THROUGH DISTANT LANDS

"I command you to be strong and courageous. Do not be afraid or dismayed because I will be there wherever you go." Are you looking for answers and guidance for your life? If you just read what you should do, everything you do will turn out well.

And just as I tell you this story, which I call a parable because of the symbolism I find in the message, I have many more adventures to say that served as revelations to understand that there was a more excellent call from above that knocked on the doors of my heart and told me that I should "die" to my past, leave everything behind; it affirmed that I was lost and invited me to open the doors of my heart to see the path of light towards victory, towards the true Home whom god had a greater purpose for me because without a doubt His ways are perfect. "For whoever wants his life will lose it, and whoever loses his life for my sake will find it." Matthew 16:25 (NKJV). Yes, it is necessary to "lose one's life," to get lost, to wander before finding the path to the light, to salvation where the welcome is providential and surpasses any situation we have gone through.

Only by confronting absence can we appreciate the reunion because it is not easy to face it without the mercy of God. Without Him, it becomes more profound amid the great chaos that exists in our lives; we feel that there is no relief or peace no matter how hard we try: it is not possible to move forward if we do not know where we are, why we do not find solutions to the immense pain we feel. Only thanks to the mercy of God can absence become light.

I believed I was in the best moment of my life for many years; I was also working tirelessly on my personal development. I had a morning plan that consisted of spending two hours reading a lot of information on how to improve my intellectual and financial life and how to have a high performance in every project that I wanted to undertake in my life for the good of my health, my physical and professional state. I had a balanced diet and exercised; I prepared myself more about business, and I even became interested in learning about the stock market. My schedule was packed, there was no time to waste, and everything was running smoothly in my personal, professional, and financial life. If I found a course out there, live or online, it was a course that I bought or enrolled in.

I will never forget that one day, that anxious search for wanting to know and learn more was the beginning of an existence that would go from being a blessing where God filled me with abundance, knowledge, and supposed earthly wisdom to a curse, a path to death without the opportunity for repentance: "For the wages of sin is death, but the gift of God is eternal life in Christ Jesus our Lord." Romans 6:23 (NKJV). And so it was, because of that desire to fill myself with multiple things that were paid for with money and superficial time, I neglected the call of God, who had already given me everything, but I abandoned it. Then everything became gloomy and dark, and there was no way to pay with money, riches, or material sacrifices for the turbulent times that came.

I remember one of my first panic attacks, a severe one, happened around 2017. At that moment, I felt like my life was leaving me. I was losing my voice, and I had a hard time breathing; I couldn't walk because of the contraction of my muscles, and while I was on my way to the emergency room I could barely whisper these words to myself: "My God, I'm not ready to leave, I still don't feel like I've

## 6. PATHS THROUGH DISTANT LANDS

fulfilled the mission for which you brought me to this life, allow me to walk your paths and not my own, let me be able to fill that void while I'm here... but if your will is to take me, I accept it."

I couldn't move my mouth or lips properly, but that's what I was saying at that moment of great despair. After accepting the situation and saying these words silently, I felt a tremendous inner peace and a sense of security and hope. I felt that there was light in that dark tunnel I was in.

The days went by, and the sensations I had experienced were very intense; the memory of that anxiety crisis kept me in a state of alert, and that terrible panic attack left me very scared and worried. There were times when I felt calm, but suddenly, something like a hurricane would come into my life, and at midnight, I would have to get up to move around the house, feel great despair, open the main door, and run out wrapped in total madness. The worst thing was that there were no doctors who could control those attacks that affected me so much; I could no longer be alone at Home, I was afraid of myself, I would pass by the kitchen and see a sharp knife, and I would stare at it, suddenly I would think again and say to myself: "But, what are you thinking? Why are you staring at that dangerous weapon? What do you want to do?" I was obsessed with that knife or any sharp object I found, but something also told me, "Don't try to do anything crazy with yourself." Later, I left my house door open during the day because that was the only way I felt safe. I thought that if something terrible happened, I would have the door open to run away, and if someone tried to hurt me, a neighbor or someone else could see or hear me and help me if necessary.

Unfortunately, human beings sometimes have to go through some setbacks not once but several times to come to their senses, but even then, we don't understand; we cling to things that we can't solve, and we want others to solve our lives for us. We blame our parents for situations that happened to us, for the way they treated us, but we don't take responsibility or give up, we don't say "Enough, I'll do what's in my hands"; because we're foolish, we don't let go of that heavy load full of resentment and envy that prevents us from returning Home victorious. Remember, giving up doesn't mean abandoning or defeating yourself, it's giving in to something bigger, more powerful than ourselves.

How often have you felt trapped by your problems, lacking the strength to move forward? Have you found yourself in a situation that seems impossible to resolve? I understand that struggle; I've been there too.

It can be incredibly challenging to accept that some situations are beyond our control. Sometimes, we find it difficult to voice our pleas to God for guidance and relief from our burdens. Accepting that we can turn to God with our problems can be hard.

The passage from Matthew 11:29-30 (NKJV) beautifully illustrates this: "Take my yoke upon you and learn from me, for I am gentle and humble in heart. You will find rest for your souls; my yoke is easy, and my burden is light." These words offer such peace and assurance, don't they? Making the courageous decision to say, "Enough; I can't do this on my own."

Humbling ourselves before God to seek His guidance is often more powerful than any therapy session, green juice, or yoga class

## 6. PATHS THROUGH DISTANT LANDS

aimed at alleviating stress and depression. It's a profound act of faith, one that can lead to true healing.

If only we would accept His help and rest in His promise.

It would be wonderful to have the wisdom to understand that things don't happen when we want them or when we think we need them but when God wants them, and it is His will. Only then will you be able to take off all the enormous weight that you feel, that you have been carrying for a long time, and have the confidence that God is there with all His power to take your burdens and control your life and affairs.

God puts numerous obstacles and signs in life so that we reconsider. The bad thing is that sometimes, the more tests we have, the more blindfolds we put on our eyes so as not to look at reality. Instead of reflecting and paying attention to the signs, we do the opposite of what could be a blessing for our lives.

We cling to doing everything our way, we insist on doing things the way we want without even taking care of the scriptures where the truth of everything is found. This happens because it is difficult to bend our knees and humbly ask God what we can do with our lives.

I share with you the answer: "Ask, and it will be given to you; seek, and you will find; knock, and it will be opened to you." Matthew 7:7 (NKJV). These biblical words are not just phrases that motivate us and say them when we are in great need; no. These words are a golden rule for our daily life.

But what happens when we violate this golden rule and only cling to God when we think we need Him when we urgently need an answer because we are in the midst of a great tribulation? There will undoubtedly be times when we do not hear His voice, and His light will not appear.

The enemy sets traps for you to stray from the proper path.

One day, I do not remember exactly how it happened, but some books that seemed new to me came into my hands with a different proposal than what I knew, and I began to read them. They spoke of many "mysteries" and things that surprised me then. They said that what we are experiencing these days is because of something that we had not resolved in "past lives" and that if we do not fix certain things in this life, we will return to another life with the same situations to fix them, and only when we finished resolving the things that we left pending would we take off that burden, and then we would be free.

I then began to read more of these kinds of works. The more I read these books, the more I realized that they belonged to the so-called New Age, a movement concerned with bringing the world into a new era of harmony and enlightenment. This trend has been very fashionable for some time.

The term "New Age" refers to a stage of love and light, which its practitioners believe will come about through transformation and healing at the individual level. According to J. Gordon Melton, director of the Institute for Studies of American Religion at the University of Virginia, "the New Age [is] seen as the vision of a New Age defined by the transformation of our broken society—characterized by poverty, war, racism, etc.—into a united community, full of abundance, peace, brotherly love..."

This movement sometimes promotes occultism, ancestral practices, communication with other spirits, and even divination; they

## 6. PATHS THROUGH DISTANT LANDS

use some meditation strategies, a lot of communication with nature, yoga, various practices for spiritual healing, work with crystals, acupuncture, acupressure, chakra healing, and Reiki or energy therapy. It's offered emotional and physical healing, among many other things, so I said to myself: "This is what I have been looking for years; here, I will find the answer to what I was looking for. If I practice all this, I will find the answers to all the questions that have always troubled me. I will have a life full of peace, be free of all ties, and finally, all this confusion that disturbs my mind and the lack of direction in my life will end."

With these ideas, I headed towards this new journey, thinking that this would end all my suffering and that this deep emptiness in my life would finally be filled. I had the idea that from then on, I would be happy and feel fulfilled. Here, I have just given you an example of my path, and I am not ashamed to say it because I want it to serve as an example and help others to get out of the lie, out of that erroneous life in which the world lives.

But no, my dear sister, brother, friend, or friend who still does not know the power of the gospel, which, just as it can come to you as a beautiful blessing, can also powerfully go to you so that you reconsider. Now, I can suggest that you never go down that path of false promises because you will only destroy your life.

When I decided to adopt certain practices of that movement, I began to feel wonder. Everything was going very well, I was happy, and I even felt more energetic, hopeful, and lighter. The weight I felt on my shoulders was lighter every day; I really wanted to be alone to connect with "My Highest Self" through meditations and breathing exercises.

# RETURN HOME

Before continuing, I must tell you to pay close attention to the following. In that apparent well-being, in that enjoyable connection with these practices, sometimes the enemy begins to enter your life. He enters in a very silent, very kind way. What happens to those who begin to use drugs or alcohol? At first, they feel happy; they feel that what they consume is filling their emptiness, and every day that passes, they want to continue consuming the same thing, then they increase the dose because they want more of that joy, of that fullness until the moment comes when they find another substance, another type of drug to experience more and more.

Then, there comes a time in their life when they find themselves so immersed in that addiction that it is challenging for them to get out of there until something supernatural and miraculous comes into their lives and helps them leave that abyss. This is how the enemy works in this deceptive world, with temporary remedies, because then the person wants more and more until they become addicted until they only manage to get hooked and feel in other dimensions. Why? Because you want to have human, earthly control over everything that happens, because you want to fix your past, control your present and even your future. That shows how my life has been, and I know the world is full of people like me.

When I started practicing the New Age movement, one day, I met someone who told me to visit a chiropractor who could adjust my bones, and with that balance, I could feel much better physically, with less stress and less depression. I didn't hesitate and went to see "this doctor." However, during the session, he started doing something that seemed very strange to me. He didn't touch my bones, but

## 6. PATHS THROUGH DISTANT LANDS

instead, he told me: "Turn toward that wall and close your eyes," so I did, and then he started to pass his hand very close to my body, without touching me, and when he went toward my chest I suddenly asked him: "What are you doing?" He answered me: "I'm going to start cleaning your chakras so that your life flows better, in harmony. Starting today, you have to come once a week."

After my first visit, I started feeling better, so I continued attending my weekly appointments. I maintained this routine for about four months, but as I kept going, I began to sense that something wasn't quite right with the process. It was during this time that he started discussing both my past and my present with me. He explained that he was a medium and possessed specific abilities. "A medium is an intermediary—someone who bridges the gap between the two worlds, with the ability to see, feel, and understand those who are no longer with us, those who exist in the afterlife," he told me. At that point, my life was in complete disarray. I felt out of control and lacked mental clarity and peace. I was living in deep despair, and my soul felt restless. I struggled with sleep and had difficulty focusing on my daily tasks.

During those days, my anxiety attacks had increased more and more; my head was spinning all the time, and the anguish I was experiencing made me believe that I was going to lose my mind soon. I asked that doctor to please not do anything to me anymore and to leave me as I was before. I felt so bad that I no longer cared if he would take away the emptiness in my life; I just wanted him to leave me as I was because before, I felt better than at that moment. Until then, I realized I was relatively happier before I found all those practices; then, my life was slipping away. I had stopped reading those books on human development, and I no longer did meditations, although there was a sign that God was coming into my life no matter what I was going through during those months.

I must confess that I did not speak about it openly, I did not say it to anyone or repeat it out loud, but in my mind, I said, "Yes, only you can save me, Almighty God, if only you would remember me and help me get out of this torture that is my days, get out of this hole in which I find myself and where I am drowning…"

I felt like I could not even breathe properly, so I walked away from that path that had promised me a false and erroneous salvation and had only doubled my anxiety and anguish. I called to cancel all the appointments I had scheduled, and I gave up on myself; defeated, I said to myself: "I will die in the midst of all this that is happening to me, or I will survive with the help of God, but I will never return to that place; nor will I remember everything I saw and heard there, everything I read and what they made me feel. I must admit that I was lost, without direction in the desert.

As incredible as it may seem, everything I experienced in that New Era was only a sign of being lost in the desert. Now I can tell you that if you, dear reader, do not know where to go, who to turn to, or who to vent to feel at peace, perhaps you are lost in the desert. So, if you are not clear about your life's purpose and are desperate because you want to find it, do not worry anymore. Many of us have gone through this, and if you have done things against the will of God, there is still time to stop your path and look for the way back Home.

## 6. PATHS THROUGH DISTANT LANDS

Now, I understand that many things had to happen for me to recognize God's strength and mercy more. I alone distanced myself from Him. I looked for immediate answers and immediate riches elsewhere. I believed in other gratifications and other powers, moving away from God, His blessings, and His path.

When I distanced myself from God, pride, vanity, and ego triumphed. I believed that with only my ability, I would achieve all my purposes, but what happened in the end was that the emptiness became bigger, desperation increased, and what they promised me were only vain hopes. Nevertheless, God was always there shepherding me like that lost sheep, and at the time, He rescued me so that I could return to His flock.

I wanted to move forward without Him. Perhaps I thought I could find my way and the path without His help, but the only thing I achieved by moving away was sinking further into the depths of the abyss. I wish with all my heart to share with you the steps I took to get out of the anguish that was leading me to madness. First, I made a fundamental decision. I said, "I have to do something now; it matters if I die trying to get out of this abyss or if this decision leads me to victory. Second, I accepted that my life was hurting me. I recognized that I had failed, hadn't done things right, and decided never to go back to the past and close the false escape routes. So, I decided to open the doors to something miraculous.

# 7

# The awakening of the heart

At times, we reflect on our lives and recognize the need for change. This desire does not stem from desperation; rather, it comes from a yearning for a life filled with greater purpose than what we have currently achieved.

If you think your life has not been easy, full of dangers, storms, and worries, your calling is more significant than you imagine. God wants to come closer to you, talk to you, give Him a space in your life, and allow Him to work in you. I tell you from the heart that it is better to heed His call than to do what I did: move away from Him, ignore Him, and believe that I was stronger and more capable than I was. Today, I recognize that I went down other dark and improper paths to look for the enemy's things. I aroused great anger, and I felt it because I could no longer find the way out to get away from those shadows, but a miracle came into my life, and He gave me the shelter I had despised again. He made me a victorious woman in the face of all the struggles I was going through. Today, I know that His great victories are:

1, victory over eternal death,

2, victory over Satan and

3, victory over the slavery of sin.

Today, I assure you that, although the physical and emotional burden may be immense, with much pain, uncertainty, and bitterness, you can emerge victorious from all these turbulent valleys.

I want to encourage you by reminding you that if your burden feels enormous and heavy, it is because your calling from God is even greater. This calling is different from the call of the world, which I once sought to please, focusing on people regardless of their actions. Take a moment to reflect on the weight of the burdens you carry—whether they are problems at Home, conflicts at work, a lack of purpose in life, struggles with depression, or a feeling that nothing is going well for you.

You may have endured great pain for a long time. Understand that these immense burdens, which can feel suffocating, carry an unbearable weight. However, they are matched by the blessings that await you. These blessings are not for those lacking patience, but for those who dive deep into their spirit. It is in those depths that you will begin to see the glory of God. In that state, He will start to shape and mold your life.

When I was deeply involved in energy healing and chakra cleansing, I regret to say that I found those pursuits to be a waste of time. They provided hollow recipes that led nowhere, often accompanied by multiple deceptions. I ended up spending a considerable amount of money on numerous charlatans who exploited our igno-

## 7. THE AWAKENING OF THE HEART

rance and the emptiness we feel in our lives. That is the world God rescued me from—one that is superficial and rife with deception.

The enemy was using me, and I had even been led to recommend the practices associated with the New Age movement. Looking back, I realize that if God had not intervened in my life and freed me from the enemy's grasp, I would have lost everything. How can I not be grateful to God for all He does for us? How can I not want Him to use me to share my testimony about what my life was like before compared to where I am now? As it says in Romans 1:16 (NKJV), "I am not ashamed of the Gospel, for it is the power of God for salvation to everyone who believes, to the Jew first and also to the Greek." I won't sugarcoat my message or just say what people want to hear without acknowledging its severity. I refuse to be complacent because living a complacent and disobedient life only distanced me from Him.

I try to say things as His Word dictates, not what most people want to read and hear. We have to know that at this time, there are people who are being used by the enemy, even Christians, because sometimes we cover our ears and blindfold ourselves to see and hear only what we want to fit in with the world and be accepted by the majority, who often live in falsehood, idolatry, with a vast emptiness in their lives and a total farce.

Currently, the world is very much into the New Age, and on many occasions, that is where the enemy hides. The devil wants to take your life away from you and keep you away from what God has prepared for you; that is why sometimes he uses these wellness traps of "spiritual healings" that only represent an investment of money disguised as messages for mental health, why do you think that in these times the remedies of this New Age are meditating, do yoga, cleanse your chakras, cleanse your house, use essential oils and crystals to heal your life. However, sincerely, my friend, all of that is not biblical; all of that is part of the work that the enemy does to take away from you what God is offering you: eternal life with Him.

Don't be fooled! Sometimes, all those therapies, all those classes that call themselves esoteric, all those potions and even drugs, those new meditations and cleansing only serve to open the doors to the devil towards a lost and hopeless life of false, unbiblical practices and doctrines, baseless invocations to wreak havoc on your life, and sometimes you knowingly let him enter your finances, your Home, to destroy the lives of your children, to make you trust and be deceived, to take away the crown that awaits you in the kingdom of God.

That is why it is essential to allow God to begin working in your life. Invite Him into your heart and Home, and He will start to shape and guide you on the path you need to follow. It is unfortunate that we often focus on clinging to God only to seek guidance for our desires—the paths that offer immediate material gratification.

We rarely ask God to mold us like clay, to undo what is damaging in our lives, to eliminate our imperfections, and to transform us so we can embrace the joy of His will. God cannot truly change our lives if we continue to walk in ways that oppose Him, seeking hollow philosophies or engaging in rituals that keep us trapped in the enemy's snares. Therefore, we must distance ourselves from these falsehoods and place our trust in Him. We should allow Him to break

## 7. THE AWAKENING OF THE HEART

us, even when it is painful, because His lessons lead to our salvation and help us learn to choose what is good. Only then will we bring Him honor and glory.

And when I say that Jesus not only lifts us, but also saves us, cleanses us, restores us, redeems us, and completely transforms our lives, I truly mean it.

I think of Angel's story. I met a young man shortly after I arrived in the United States. He was a good kid and a dedicated student, perhaps not the brightest, but always willing to give his best effort. He was impulsive and full of dreams. He enjoyed playing basketball in the yards, behind the plastic factories, and chatting with the girls who worked in the meatpacking plants after school. He often sought someone to talk to, especially a girl he liked a lot named Maria. She was a thin girl with curly hair who always seemed to silently accompany a group of young girls in their factory uniforms.

Angel spent his days studying, working odd jobs, and trying to make friends. He had moved to the United States with his parents when he was very young, and felt he had adapted to the local customs of the neighborhood boys. Time passed in this way, but perhaps his lack of confidence led him to associate with "friends" who encouraged him to consume alcohol and try other drugs. At first, Angel hesitated. He was somewhat afraid of becoming involved in that lifestyle. However, since everyone he knew was gathering at parties that lasted for hours—drinking and seemingly indifferent to their surroundings—he eventually gave in. He began attending these gatherings more frequently, enjoying conversations with others and dancing with girls, mostly his classmates from school.

One day, he was invited to a party near the end of the school semester. His friends urged him to stay longer, but he wanted to go Home to finish some pending schoolwork. The party was lively, with music that filled the room, encouraging the dancing and laughter of the boys. While Angel wanted to enjoy the festivities, he also knew that if he stayed, he wouldn't make any progress on his assignments the next day. He told his friends that he should leave, emphasizing that he needed to complete his schoolwork and submit it on time. He never imagined that that night would change his life forever.

His friends insisted that he stay, offering him more drinks, but Angel maintained that he wouldn't be able to complete his tasks the next day. Looking mischievously at the others, one of his friends approached Angel and said that he could help him avoid feeling lazy or hungover the following day. Angel, already feeling dizzy, asked how that was possible. His friend told him to follow him so he could show him how to regain his energy and avoid feeling tired. He also assured Angel that whenever he had something important to do, he could use what he would give him to feel strong, motivated, and happy.

Angel was intrigued; he didn't quite understand what his friend meant by feeling motivated and energized. He followed him into a room, and behind came another boy who was carrying a light leather backpack. One of Angel's friends leaned against the door to prevent anyone from entering, while the friend who had convinced Angel said to the boy with the backpack, "We want you to give him something to keep him energized. Don't worry about the cost; I'll take care of it. He's my friend..."

## 7. THE AWAKENING OF THE HEART

That's how it all started. Angel became addicted to cocaine, and then he looked for harder drugs. If he had to take an exam, he would first look for a line of coke; if he were looking for a job, he would do coke to dance all night and get closer to the girl he liked; a few drinks of alcohol were no longer enough; with coke, he felt safe, brave, funny. He used it every evening, then from the morning, in a few months he looked haggard, impatient, distressed, only after consuming it did he seem a little relieved. But coke was no longer enough, alcohol even less; he looked for more substances and tolerated them less. He left school, he lost the jobs he found very quickly, and one day, he found himself lost in the street, without money, without drugs or friends.

He looked for a place to calm his addiction and spend the night. He wanted to rest, but his nervousness made him see things, get irritated by everything, and feel like his chest was tearing. He walked for a long time until he came to a bridge where several people were staggering or lying on the ground or talking. Angel was desperate. He approached a group of boys who were quarreling to ask them for drugs, and they looked at him with disdain. He walked a few steps and saw a young woman lying on the ground, leaning on a red imitation leather bag where she had her belongings. The girl was wearing tennis shoes in good condition and was covered by a blue jacket resembling a brand name. The first thing Angel thought about was to snatch her things and run. They would give him something for them.

He was sweating, and felt his heart racing in his chest, pounding so loudly that in his desperation, he thought he could actually hear the violent beats. When looking into the darkness of the tunnel; no one was nearby. The rats were approaching the puddles, and at the slightest noise, they would scurry away through the eroded cement. Angel approached with his hands clenched. He gave the woman a light kick to check if she was deeply asleep or heavily drugged. The girl did not move. Cautiously, he stepped closer, his eyes were wide with fear, felt horrible tremors in his hands and a wave of desperation. He tugged hard at the jacket and the bag, but the girl clung to them tightly. He knew he couldn't turn back. He yanked on the bag again, convinced he would find something of value to sell. Suddenly, the woman reacted as if she were having convulsions; she growled, clinging to her belongings, writhed, and screamed at him to leave her alone. Then, she looked at him, and in terror, he could only say, "Maria!"

From that day forward, Angel made a determined effort to overcome his addictions. It required a significant amount of work for him to quit drugs and begin a new life. He had to accept that he had turned away from God, seeking instead a false diversion in drugs and alcohol—an artificial paradise that caused him to lose respect for himself and for others. Now, he is committed to repairing the damage he has done and understands that, while he cannot change the past, he can take responsibility for his actions in the present.

He expresses that God allowed him to see again, walk again, and believe again. Even though he had forgotten about God, God, in His infinite mercy, never abandoned him. He confesses that it pained him deeply to find Maria in such a situation, and he realized that wanting to rob her was not just about taking her belongings; it was about harming an innocent person. However, God provided him a way to escape that moment and helped him understand that he could

## 7. THE AWAKENING OF THE HEART

transform his life. Since then, he has committed himself to that journey of change into his evolutionary path.

I'm sure Angel's story resonates with many of us because we all might know someone who is struggling with a similar situation, or perhaps we have faced the challenges of addiction ourselves. It's no secret that life is filled with insecurities, setbacks, traps, and uncertainties. Many of us have endured significant pain along our journeys, and some have stumbled upon addictions or other dangers.

I understand what you are going through because I have experienced many of these struggles. You might have traversed dark valleys and walked long distances through barren lands. For years, you may have felt as though you were lost in a distant, freezing, and dark place, unable to find your way back Home. I also know that you long for that return because great welcoming, security, and understanding await you. Someone is waiting to give you that powerful hug that will make you feel everything is alright, to let you know that He was only waiting to provide you with protection, guidance, and the security that you had lost.

Perhaps you are longing to feel welcome at Home, and I want you to know that I understand. As I write these words, I think of you and everyone who reads this. I know the places you have traveled and the struggles you are facing because I have experienced them too. It does not matter how old you are—whether you are young or old, a man or a woman—I feel your pain. I have also crossed the desert in complete darkness. I have been lost and have had a broken soul. Today, I want to accompany you on your journey back Home and help you in any way I can so that you arrive safely at your final destination.

## RETURN HOME

As I write these reflections, I am overwhelmed by intense emotions and a strong heartbeat. I had to pause for a moment because I couldn't hold back my tears. Writing this brings me to the time I wandered through the desert, when I felt helpless day and night. I searched aimlessly, moving from side to side without finding peace, consolation, or hope. Yes, like Angel, I was lost and sorrowful.

I may not know you personally or have any details about your story, but I am certain of one thing: "You are a very loved person." I want to share with you that someone is waiting for you with open arms, ready to give you a warm, powerful hug that will wipe away all your tears. He will not ask where you've been, why you left, why it took you so long, or why you forgot about Him. All He wants is for you to feel safe. He wants you to know that nothing else in your life matters as much as what you'll feel during that incredible encounter. You won't need anyone to tell you that everything will be fine, that you have tremendous potential, or that you will achieve everything you set out to do. Those reassurances will be unnecessary because the warm embrace you will receive upon your return Home will be more than enough.

You will come to realize that you were never truly alone on your journey. Someone was always there, waiting for you and understanding everything you went through. Even if your path was the most complicated, darkest, and coldest, there was a presence watching over you, awaiting the moment you would accept and declare, "I have traveled this far alone. I will no longer walk without God by my side. I will return to Him, to His arms and love, to that first love,

## 7. THE AWAKENING OF THE HEART

and I will stay in His House to witness the wonders He will perform in my life and with my loved ones." In that moment, you will have the chance to say to Him, "I have finally arrived at your Home, so please do with me as you will."

# 8

# El llamado

God places us in unique situations for special reasons. It is true that God creates paths even when it seems impossible to move forward, guiding us through the most unexpected circumstances. Remember the words: "You have made known to me the paths of life; You will fill me with joy in Your presence" (Acts 2:28, NKJV). You may have doubts, feel skeptical, or lack interest in a divine calling, and I understand that; I do not judge you for it. I don't aim to convince you of anything, either. I simply want to share something from my own experience.

I didn't see any of this coming. Caught up in my meaningless existence, it felt like I was just wandering aimlessly, walking around with my eyes covered. Perhaps I didn't care anymore about finding a way out of my situation; maybe I had grown tired of begging, of crying, and even of living.

I felt so lost that I didn't realize I had been wandering without purpose for many years. My body was exhausted from this futile journey, and the more I continued down that path, the more I felt myself sinking deeper into confusion and despair. It was as if I were desperately trying to move forward in the middle of a desert, overwhelmed by suffering and uncertainty. I don't know if you've ever walked in a desert, but I had the opportunity to do so in the deserts of Dubai. With each step I took, I experienced a sense of distance, confusion, and isolation. The finer the sand, the more I sank with every step. I hoped that with each new step, I would find firmer ground, but instead, I just sank deeper into the sand. I realized that in this vast expanse, I was only moving away from any possibility of progress, making it increasingly difficult to return. Even when the guides advised me to follow the footprints in the sand, it was nearly impossible to walk properly. This was my experience, and it was incredibly challenging to leave that place that seemed limitless.

When I finally arrived at the hotel, I felt my feet could take no more. The pain was unbearable; sometimes, walking felt nearly impossible after trudging through the sand. I drank a liter of water to quench my thirst and collapsed into bed from sheer exhaustion. It had been an overwhelming struggle to navigate that place, and I felt I had made little progress.

We often find ourselves stuck in difficult situations, similar to wandering in a barren desert where prosperity seems impossible. We continue to force our way along dark and gloomy paths, searching for signs and hoping that things will eventually improve. Despite feeling increasingly trapped, we persist with the same strategies, stubbornly ignoring the reality of our circumstances and the destructive choices we've made. We refuse to acknowledge that there is a better way to live—a way that leads to true victory in all we do. Many believers

## 8. THE CALL

share this mindset: no matter the challenges we face, with God's help, we will ultimately achieve victory.

I was deeply attached to what I saw and to my beliefs in superficial philosophies. I relied on the words of those I had taken as my teachers or spiritual guides, who merely surrounded me with empty speeches and hollow promises. The truth is, I was also in pursuit of temporary satisfaction and immediate pleasures—just like the fast-paced demands of today's world where everyone wants everything instantly.

It's truly curious how we find a sense of immediacy in everything around us. Places even bear names that reflect this rush—like "fast food"—because that is what people desire: quick, easy solutions that can be attained without much thought. We often pursue these shortcuts, ignoring whether they are genuinely beneficial or harmful to our health. There are countless advertisements for things like "lose 10 pounds in 10 days," promising rapid results.

For years, I lived this way, chasing false promises. I lacked the patience to wait for what was meant for me. Instead, I ventured through life, seeking to attain my desires as quickly as possible, which only led me deeper into despair. My focus was solely on the tangible, on what I could touch with my hands, rather than on what can only be perceived through spiritual insight. As it is written, "Therefore, we do not fix our eyes on what is seen, but on what is not seen. For what is seen is temporary, but what is not seen is eternal." (2 Corinthians 4:18, NKJV).

For quite some time, I felt a strong sense that there was something I needed to do—something that no one else could do for me.

# RETURN HOME

I kept hearing a faint voice telling me not to seek answers elsewhere, as I wouldn't find what I was looking for. I sensed that my time was limited, and I didn't have much space to contemplate the situation. "Behold, I stand at the door and knock. If anyone hears My voice and opens the door, I will come in to him and will dine with him, and he with Me." — Revelation 3:20 (NKJV). This verse felt like a message urging me to cross over the Jordan, suggesting that on the other side, I would find everything I had been searching for.

I sought my Home, a place of rest and light, where I could dwell in that promised land. As I listened and looked in all directions, I dreamed of the call to guide me back to where He had once brought me. It felt as though a protective shadow accompanied each of the steps I took. Sometimes, I sensed that everything in my life was on pause, and something was urging me to recognize that there lay a better opportunity waiting for me just beyond. All I needed to do was pay attention and heed the call to embrace this new opportunity for my life. How many of you are also searching for a "new opportunity"?

I felt a profound calling deep within my heart and gut, but for some reason, I didn't embrace it. By human nature, we tend to cling to what is visible. We believe in what we can touch and follow the actions of most people around us. Often, we fail to believe in the invisible, the eternal, and the things that come from above.

I remember the first time I was in that Islamic country I told you about: Iran. When I lived in Tehran, one morning, I was sitting on my bed. It was 5:01 AM, and I hadn't gone to sleep yet when suddenly the call to the first prayer of the day, known as Fajr, began to sound.

# 8. THE CALL

That call in Arabic was so loud that I felt it echo off the walls of my Home. That morning was extraordinary for me. I felt that this call was not only meant for the Islamic people but also a personal call for me—not to convert to Islam, but to return to the promises I had made to God. It was a powerful, profound, and beautiful experience, as if I were being summoned back Home.

That prayer from the people of Tehran felt like a direct message from God, clear and beautiful, saying, "Come back to me, and I will return to you. You will realize everything you have lost while away from Home." I understood that God was reaching out to me in this unexpected place. It felt like a miracle that I was awake so far from Home at five in the morning.

In that particular morning, the call to prayer, which was supposed to last only about two minutes, transformed into an eternal and unforgettable resonance in my heart. Suddenly, I felt my whole body shake, overwhelmed by emotions I could hardly explain. I struggled to comprehend how such a divine moment could be happening to me, and then I burst into tears. These were truly intense emotions that words cannot capture. I felt the call to prayer deeply, and my body responded with a bristling sensation.

I felt God's presence, and my tears were a mix of astonishment, gratitude, strangeness, and humble joy. Everything felt profoundly strange, as if my world was collapsing to make way for a new life built on something solid and enduring.

Those songs were something truly special, and I must confess that despite their Muslim essence, I never had any confusion about my beliefs. When I heard a call to prayer, I perceived it as a call from my God, the only God in all of human history. He is the one who founded the heavens and the earth. "Hear, O Israel: The Lord our God, the Lord, is one." (Deuteronomy 6:4, NKJV).

At that moment, I bowed down in His presence, got on my knees, and began to pray. I begged God to come into my life, acknowledging that I had forgotten to praise Him, the living God. I pleaded for His acceptance, understanding that I had not maintained a close relationship with Him for a long time. It was then when I felt an overwhelming desire to have a personal relationship with the God I had encountered long ago.

I made a promise to serve Him every day of my life because I realized I had failed Him and struggled to find a way back. I missed the relationship I once had with God and longed for that connection again. I carried a heavy emptiness that felt burdensome, but now it was time to unload that weight and allow something new to fill the void in my life. At that moment, I felt awakened—a constant need for Him. Although I didn't understand everything immediately, I knew I needed to leave my past behind, get back on the right path, and let my old life fade away to make room for a new beginning.

I came to understand the importance of humility during a significant moment in my life. I realized that in the presence of something greater than myself, I felt utterly insignificant, overwhelmed by my own pride and ego. In that moment, I humbled myself and opened my heart to a higher purpose that could illuminate my life. I was faced with the opportunity for a new beginning, but I knew I could not live two lives at once. To embrace this new life in Christ, I had to let go of my former life of darkness and despair. This leads to

## 8. THE CALL

one of the greatest dangers and mistakes we Christians often make: we want to live life on our own terms while expecting God to intervene for us when it suits our needs.

We desire His guidance and miracles, but still aim to navigate our existence by relying solely on our own plans. When burdens arise, we often turn to doctors, psychiatrists, or psychologists for relief. I have nothing against these health professionals; however, too often we seek quick fixes without addressing deeper, more profound spiritual needs. We overlook the divine and the blessings that come from above. In times of family crises, we might confide in friends or neighbors who may even be grappling with their own serious issues, asking for their support instead of seeking a more profound understanding and internal guidance.

The same applies to the search for a "purpose in life." People often approach me for counseling, wanting me to provide answers or suggestions for their careers or business ventures. I realize now that my responses were often filled with empty platitudes. Today, I recognize that without humility, we cannot progress in life. If we do not humble ourselves before His presence, we will miss His calling and fail to see His glory. If you find yourself longing to return Home, remember that your current struggles are not coincidental.

At this moment, He invites us to honor His presence and seek Him in spirit and truth. Therefore, I urge you not to attempt to shoulder the heavy burdens you have carried for years on your own. Instead, humbly come before Him, leave your past behind, kneel down, and sincerely cry out for guidance. Seek the best counselor, the greatest healer, the truest friend—because He will lead you to where you truly belong. Make the decision to embark on a direct, uninterrupted journey to God; He does not require intermediaries. Remember, many times, we desire instant results on our terms, but that is not how true encounters with the divine occur.

Remember, if you are experiencing significant suffering and cannot find a way out, it is not merely a coincidence. Everything happens for a reason. The greater our difficulties, the greater our calling. God is reaching out to you; He is knocking at the doors of your heart. Will you open them?

# 9

# Dying to live

When we deeply feel the need for a new life and significant transformation, it's important to recognize that such change cannot occur while we remain in our current state. Often, we must endure challenging experiences and be willing to let go of our "old self" to embrace a new life, which can only be found in Christ Jesus. This transformation is not merely about making superficial lifestyle changes that are often discussed in the world; it represents a profound and unimaginable calling. It requires us to rethink, speak, and act differently.

As soon as problems arise, we should view them from a new perspective. Therefore, the transformation in your daily life and in your life, Cristina, starts with you. It's not about having the power to transform your own life, but rather being proactive and taking responsibility for that change, being obedient, and recognizing that the journey begins with you—nobody else can do it for you. Our heavenly Father is gracious in granting us free will; He does not desire anything from us by force, but rather through our own choice. I want to emphasize that when you look in the mirror, remember that the transformation in your life begins with you.

Once you acknowledge this, entrust your life to God, for He will shape it like a potter molding clay, working to fulfill His purpose for your transformation. It's true that He longs for you to return Home, but His call extends beyond simply restoring the empty, deceitful life you previously had. He aims to extract you from the darkness that confines you, where you are consumed by your own desires and live without life or hope. He wants to lead you to His side, lifting your burdens and suffering, to a new life filled with hope and illumination. If we are not fully committed to Him, then we are not truly present. We cannot be divided in His presence. I confess that during the most intense moments when I felt a strong need for a loving relationship with my Father, I often sought that relationship for my own convenience, without being willing to sacrifice anything for Him. This realization is disheartening, but it's true, and I will reiterate it as many times as necessary in case there are others who feel the same.

Many people, perhaps thousands, have experienced similar feelings, keeping them hidden deep within their hearts. Yes, you may ask God to come to you, to help you, and to nurture a relationship with Him, but you may be doing so from a distance! You hesitate to draw closer, fearing that this closeness will demand more from you than you are willing to give. We often wish to maintain our existing lifestyles while seeking different outcomes, but that is not how it works. True change requires a real commitment.

The truth is that we are often unwilling to pay the fair price to be in His presence, allowing Him to work in our lives. We must be very

## 9. DYING TO LIVE

clear about this: if we expect a lot from Him, we must be willing to give everything—yes, everything. We need to leave behind our old ways of being, speaking, and even how we relate to the world. We must let that empty way of existing die in order to fully embrace a new life with God.

"The sun shines for everyone, but the shadow of the Almighty is only for those who choose to enter the shelter of the Most High." (Psalm 91:1). This means that you will have to die in order to truly live. "That which was is already; and that which is to be has already occurred; and God restores what is past." (Ecclesiastes 3:15). Does this make sense to you?

Let me share my experience. It was a time when felt dead in life, trapped in a state of complete emotional, spiritual, and physical blockage, unable to find a place where my soul could truly rest. The only things I could touch and feel were material possessions because my life was filled with vanity, lacking the real flavors of nature or spirituality. Now, reflecting on this, a verse comes to mind that I often heard when I was younger in the house of God: "Remember your Creator in the days of your youth, before the difficult days come and the years draw near when you will say, 'I have no pleasure in them.'" (Ecclesiastes 12:1, KJV). I must admit that when I first heard these words, they didn't touch my heart, and I never imagined they would resonate in my life as they do now.

It seems God was telling me to pay attention, for difficult times would come my way. After much reflection, I came to a realization: "Yes, I have no joy in my life; I feel empty and lost in the world." In that moment of introspection, a voice emerged before me and said, "You will have to die to live."

At the time, I didn't fully understand it, and often, these words would come to my mind. Then, suddenly, the spirit of God descended upon my life. In that moment, I realized that I had to leave behind "my old self," and I grasped what "dying to live" truly meant. I had never thought that these words would hold such profound meaning and would forever mark my existence. I understood that this "dying" would signal the end of all my traumas, of the immense emptiness in my life, of my anxieties, and of being unfaithful to God. It would mark the conclusion of my lack of direction, paving the way for a new beginning in search of new horizons.

It was incredible to discover that while I was just beginning to comprehend everything that had happened, God already had a plan in place to open a bright path for me to return Home. God was aware of my anguish, my losses, my loneliness, and my emptiness. I came to realize that all I had experienced was a call from Him to repent.

God instructed me that I needed to die in order to be reborn and to live a new life free of all ties. I discovered that everything I had done was in vain: all those books I had read about self-improvement and achieving success were merely superficial reflections. All the self-help courses I had taken and everything I had accumulated financially had led to nothing. In that moment, I recognized that I was back in the divine call: "Do not store up for yourselves treasures on earth, where moth and rust destroy, and where thieves break in and steal; but store up for yourselves treasures in heaven, where neither moth nor rust destroys, and where thieves do not break in nor steal. For where your treasure is, there your heart will be also." (Luke 12:32-34 NKJV).

## 9. DYING TO LIVE

I then understood that my focus was now directed toward something far greater and deeper than earthly possessions. My gaze had shifted to a higher purpose, close to that treasure I sensed I was about to discover, even though I did not truly know what it would be. One thing was clear: whatever I found would be miraculous.

Now, let me share with you something that relates to my understanding of "you have to die to live."

One night, I had a dream that provided clues about where a treasure might be hidden, apparently in my birthplace. In the dream, I saw myself gazing at a mine of money in space and looking down at the Earth. While I observed that treasure buried just a few meters below the surface, I noticed that I didn't feel any joy about knowing its location. Instead, my only concern was grappling with the responsibility that came with understanding what should be done with that buried treasure. I wondered what accounts I would have to render upon taking possession, as I realized that a price had to be paid to truly enjoy that treasure and its benefits. Thus, my dream unfolded, filled with indecision, as I wrestled with how to proceed without getting tangled up in complications from acquiring such vast wealth. Yes, it was an enormous treasure—but it would also carry a significant responsibility.

How many people in the world are millionaires, carrying many treasures and great responsibilities—not only to themselves but also to society, debtors, and creditors? On the other hand, there are those who have no money and do not worry about it, lacking responsibility to anyone and sometimes not even to themselves.

While I dreamed of having a great treasure, I sensed that something significant was about to enter my life—an important and valuable miracle that would come with great responsibility to handle that treasure correctly. I share this because I want to tell you something that still amazes me to this day.

One day, out of nowhere, a beautiful lion appeared in my backyard. Yes, you read that correctly! A magnificent lion that initially filled me with immense fear, as I had never seen one up close, let alone in my own Home. This incredible animal stayed on my property for three days.

To this day, I don't know how it ended up there, especially since my house is completely fenced and well-protected with no way for anyone to get in. Yet, there was that beautiful lion, looking around with an imposing presence, its gaze calm and gentle, moving through my yard as if it truly belonged there.

When I told people about the lion outside my house, they suggested it was a sign that something of great value was coming to me. I humbly reminded myself, "I know; that's what I feel. It's time to prepare myself, for what is coming is not monetary but a gift from above—a treasure that will restore everything I have lost. It must be something great and majestic." I affirmed this to myself, not swayed by others' opinions because I don't believe in superstitions.

I felt that all the hardships I had endured were coming to an end; something within me was dying, and my earthly desires were fading away, along with the weight of my failures and difficult moments. I realized I needed to make room for what was to come, for that great event that was about to unfold.

Without making space for something more valuable, how could we receive meaningful things in our lives? That's why I now invite

## 9. DYING TO LIVE

you to eliminate, withdraw, abandon, and let go of everything that no longer serves your spiritual life—everything that keeps you from an existence that transcends and leaves behind false promises and empty temptations.

It is important to break down the structures in your life that cling to superficial things, vanity, and selfishness. By making the decision to abandon these elements and allow certain aspects of my life to collapse, I have come to understand, much like in the Book of Job 14:1-22, the brevity of life. I felt as though my world was falling apart around me; I felt exposed and aimlessly running from side to side in a vast desert, engulfed in darkness. I struggled to find even the faintest light, let alone the path to the truth I sensed calling me softly. I realized that if I couldn't hear that calling clearly, it was because I was still distracted by worldly concerns that made it difficult to pay attention to God's voice, which guides us towards clarity.

We often fail to hear His voice because we cling so tightly to the enormous burdens we carry, which weigh heavily upon us like a mountain.

As we drag ourselves through life, we remain aware that at any moment, these burdens could crash down on us, leaving us trapped. This was my experience. I was deeply afraid to let go of everything old, terrified of stepping into the unknown. I didn't pay attention to God's voice, which urged me to release my burdens and allow everything in my life to collapse. He wanted to show me that He would be there to care for and protect me.

When that mountain eventually fell, God would catch me in His embrace, helping me cross over to the other side of the Jordan, leading me to the promised land He had prepared for me. What a beautiful promise! And God would be with me, saying: "When you pass through the waters, I will be with you; if you pass through the rivers, they will not overwhelm you; when you pass through the fire, you will not be burned, nor will the flame scorch you."

I now clearly realize that if we do not allow that mountain to collapse—no matter how much we fear it—nothing new will come into our lives. I invite you to stand firm before God and not shy away from what He can do for you. Let everything unfold under His will; if you run away, nothing will change. But if you stay and trust in His plan, everything will happen as He intended.

During the emotional turmoil I experienced, there were moments when I could be calm, sitting in my dining room with a cup of hot tea, and suddenly feel my spirit escaping me, rising while my body remained prostrate in the chair. I didn't fully understand what was happening then. In desperation, my soul tried to return.

Now I understand that it wasn't just me making that effort to reclaim my spirit; it was the divine power of God telling me, "It's not your time yet. Allow certain things to die so I can make you new again. Let me mold you, be with you, and walk alongside you."

I clung tightly to my past, but holding on did nothing to stop God from working in my life. I became a poor vessel for His noble purposes, leading me into deep crises.

The hospital became my second Home as I frequently visited the emergency room. There were even times when they suggested sending me to a psychiatric facility because the emotional struggles I faced felt overwhelming, leading me to call 911 in desperation, be-

## 9. DYING TO LIVE

lieving I was dying. It may sound dramatic, but I was living a spiritual war—a battle similar to those that God often confronts with the enemy. After many falls, fears, and painful experiences, I emerged from that war victorious. When we close the door on the enemy, we find true victory in Christ Jesus.

We must celebrate our victories, approach God with humility, and make a firm promise never to abandon Him. We should always be attentive to the signs He sends us, as they will undoubtedly carry something beneficial for us.

I assure you, dear reader, that you have likely received divine signs at some point in your life. That is why I urge you to pay attention: while the sun shines for everyone, the shadow of the Almighty is reserved for those who choose to enter the shelter of the Most High. This requires a willingness to "die" to our old selves in order to truly live. As stated in Ephesians 4:22 (NKJV), "As for the former way of life, put off the old man who is corrupt according to deceitful desires, and be renewed in the spirit of your mind; and put on the new man, created according to God in righteousness and holiness of truth."

We need to leave our old lives behind and be reborn, like newborn children who must learn everything anew. I realized that the "I" — the beautiful treasure God created, which He has known since before I entered this world — had been buried deep within me, and He was calling me to wake from that deep sleep. I understood how He had been by my side since childhood, and throughout the different stages of my life, even until the present. Yet, caught up in earthly ambitions, false illusions, vanities, and the traps of my ego, I was blind to His presence and neglectful of His call.

I had become accustomed to walking in darkness and was afraid of the light and the truth. To embrace them spiritually, I needed to start over, like a child learning to walk for the first time. I had fallen into the trap of believing that the life I was leading was the right one, but I began to question why. Perhaps you, who are reading this, are wondering the same thing. This belief stemmed from what parents, relatives, friends, and society taught us: that the broad path most of the world walks is the true one, filled with banality, deceptions, false beliefs, and the struggles of the ego centered around material wealth and vanity.

That was my life — entangled in earthly distractions that overwhelmed me and made it easy to lose my way. Adding to this were the traumas of my childhood, which in adolescence led me from one person to another, from supposed experts to gurus, seeking guidance that proved useless in my quest for a fulfilling life.

I spent many years going in circles, treating my life like clay that I could mold in my own flawed way, ultimately harming myself. Eventually, I believe God said, "That's enough. Wait, stop! Let me mold you according to my design so you can see the supernatural truth and distinguish the actions of the One who can do all things." Although I am not certain of His exact words, what I do know is that He treated me in a way I had never experienced before. I thought I was living my last days when, in reality, that was the beginning of a deeper molding process. If the clay does not give itself completely, the potter cannot create anything meaningful from it.

When I finally answered His call, I felt like I was dying; my physical body seemed to be leaving this world. However, what God

## 9. DYING TO LIVE

was doing with His strength was letting that sense of "I" die. I was leaving everything behind as He transformed my way of living, thinking, and being. This process allowed me to present myself before His presence as He desired, helping me discover my purpose in life. I experienced a profound rebirth that resonated through every nerve in my body, enabling me to rise from the depths of my previous state.

In the Bible, it is written: "Therefore He says: Awake, you who sleep, and arise from the dead, and Christ will give you light." (Ephesians 5:14, NKJV). When He awakens and you arise, Christ, like the light, will illuminate your life, guiding you on the right path and filling you with His grace and truth. That is why it is so important to let the old self die, so you can be enlightened and no longer live in darkness.

# 10

# From being lost to being found

Today, more than ever, this phrase resonates: the work of God has been completed, and now it must be revealed! "The Spirit of the Lord God is upon me; because the Lord has anointed me. He has sent me to preach good news to the depressed, to bind up the brokenhearted, to proclaim liberty to the captives, and the opening of the prison to those who are bound; to proclaim the acceptable year of the Lord and the day of vengeance of our God, to comfort all who mourn; to appoint to those who mourn in Zion, to give them beauty for ashes, the oil of joy for mourning, a garment of praise for the spirit of heaviness; and they shall be called trees of righteousness, the planting of the Lord, that He may be glorified." — Isaiah 61:1-3 (NKJV).

Everything has a reason and a purpose. God never makes mistakes; He is patient with each one of us. Even though we commit ourselves to serve Him and glorify His name, we often fail Him. There are times when we spend years without being in His presence, neglecting to glorify Him, and it may seem like we've forgotten that He is always there—ready and able to change our lives in the blink of an eye. Just as a lightning bolt can destroy our lives, God can also come like a lightning bolt to give us life, new opportunities, and eternal life. He has a wonderful plan of salvation, although we frequently choose to walk through the desert of our own making. This path can be painful and difficult, yet we pursue it because we believe we know what is best for us.

Mistakenly and foolishly, we follow our own desires, seeking that much-desired Home, only to find ourselves lost in baseless beliefs that divert us from returning to Him. Sunk in material pretensions, we often forget that this world of appearances is not our true Home; we are merely passengers. We resist accepting that someone knows our paths better and is patiently waiting for us to return to His presence. "For my yoke is easy, my burden is light." (St. Matthew 11:30, NKJV).

It is only when we release our burdens to Him that He can work in our lives. How can we expect His help if we are too busy carrying heavy suitcases? We focus so much on bearing the weight that we lose sight of what is truly important. His word teaches that He hides things from the wise and reveals them to children—those who are lost, those who wander aimlessly in the dark, and those who are just beginning to walk, talk, and eat.

We must understand that we are all new creatures. Everything from our past has been forgotten and buried. When you chose to be with Him, you left your old way of living behind; you eliminated everything superficial that was no longer useful to you.

Now, you are ready to walk and live in the light because everything has become new. Just allow Him to take control of your life so that He can manifest Himself along your path and show you what He

## 10. FROM BEING LOST TO BEING FOUND

desires for you. Then, it will no longer be about your way, but about His timing and His methods in designing the destiny He has prepared for you. I want to share a wonderful experience I had, one that I still find difficult to understand sometimes.

One Sunday morning, around seven or seven-thirty in March 2023, I was awakened by a wave of electricity that surged through my entire body. It was intense and inexplicable. This surge traveled from my head to my toes, touching every cell in my body and breaking through all my nerves. What I experienced at that moment was both amazing and terrifying. I was fully awake, feeling everything perfectly—it wasn't a nightmare. Even now, when I think about it, I realize I went through something entirely supernatural, and I still lack the human capacity to comprehend it fully.

In all my life, I had never heard, read, or seen anything like it—not even in a movie. I never felt the need to discuss it with anyone; it felt too profound. It was a moment just between me and my heavenly Father, a relationship akin to having Him as my family doctor. Every second, I found myself asking, "Father God, why is this happening? What are you trying to teach me? What do You want from me? Where do You want me to go? Where are You taking me?" These questions became endless.

That time, when that wave of electricity covered me completely, deep inside, I thought it was the end of my life because that force was potent. I felt that it was breaking not only my bones but also my muscles, my tendons, and all the cells in my body, and the most terrible thing is that I could not find any reason for what was happening to me. My human strength was leaving me; I was losing my life, and at that moment, I had no way to ask for help. I knew no human power could help me, not even calling 911. Could I ask for help, as I did every time I had panic attacks or when I felt that my physical body was present, but I felt that my spirit was flying in search of its Home? No, at that moment, I couldn't get help with the task, although I must admit that even the last few times I asked for help, my support was no longer enough.

I remember that I only heard the very low voices of the doctors saying to each other and the nurses that I was not in my right mind. And on this occasion, when my body was lying on the bed, it seemed as if I were taking my last breaths because the electric waves were going on for an eternity, and the end was not coming.

I confess I didn't know then that all that breaking of bones, tendons, neurons, and all the body's cells happened because God was making me whole again! He was letting that human die completely to offer me a new life; he was shaping my existence in his way. In those conditions I could not move, I could not open my eyes, much less speak, although the strange thing is that I did feel my body moving through that electric wave, I could feel that, I felt my brain tense and the force running through me to the tips of my toes.

Finally, the electric current stopped. After feeling that violent wave, a light emerged that surrounded my head to give me peace after the storm, tranquility after years that I spent suffering, confused, full of pain and hate as if it were a sign of relief that everything would be okay. I felt that I would no longer be in the darkness; God had taken me out of that sinful path, and I was in his presence to contemplate his beauty and live in the light, no longer in darkness. I remember that

## 10. FROM BEING LOST TO BEING FOUND

I could not see that light with my human, carnal, earthly eyes; it was a beautiful vision that I could only observe with my spiritual eyes; in my mind, I looked at it and only said: "In the name of Jesus Christ, in the name of Jesus Christ, in the name of Jesus Christ!" Only those words came out of my mouth; that was my new vocabulary.

As a human being, I struggle to find the words to describe the experience that transformed my life that morning. I have never encountered anything in books or documentaries that could adequately capture what happened to me. My only request to God is that you, who have yet to experience this light, may one day encounter its transformative power, capable of erasing all your suffering and allowing you to bask in its brilliance.

"My God, grant me the words to convey to my friends—those who do not yet know You, or who have forgotten You—that they have lost their way in the darkness of this world. Please turn on that light for them so they can find their way back Home. Your light is astonishing; it cannot be compared to the brilliance of any diamond or gold this earthly life has to offer. The beauty of the light You revealed to me covers all sin, all evil thoughts, and all suffering and darkness."

This majestic light illuminates everything, eventually reaching Your holy kingdom. This experience surpasses any joy I have known in my earthly life. That light provides just a tiny glimpse of what awaits us if we choose to return Home, following You to serve, honor, and exalt Your name. My remaining days will never be enough to express my gratitude for the gift of light You bestowed upon me—a beautiful light so bright that it can penetrate any darkness and illuminate any situation more brilliantly than any imagined rainbow.

The light that surrounded me was majestic, a dazzling display of a thousand colors, resembling a rainbow, accompanied by a soothing hum that calmed my spirit. It felt as though that hum was neutralizing some burdens in my life. As electric waves coursed through my body, the magnificent light continued enveloping me, and suddenly, I felt words reach my being. I silently expressed them; my spirit spoke: "In the name of Jesus Christ… in the name of Jesus Christ… in the name of Jesus Christ…" Those were the only words my soul could articulate—the only phrase that God placed upon my lips. They were words I hadn't spoken in many years, yet I realized how beautiful they are. These words encompass everything; they fulfill everything.

I sensed that a powerful and glorious force was telling me, "If you don't say them, I will make you say them." That is how extraordinarily powerful He is when He manifests in our lives, often in ways we may not expect. He has remarkable and inexplicable ways of touching our hearts majestically. That's why, now more than ever, dear friend and sister reading my story, I urge you: the greatest loss in life is to end your days without ever knowing the promises He has for you. I humbly share my experience with you because I hope to help you awaken from that deep sleep and seek Christ now. He is always available to begin a relationship with you, offering you the eternal gifts He has in store.

As I write these words, my soul overflows with joy—an indescribable joy that cannot be compared to anything material in this world. It is an extraordinary joy, difficult to explain, but one thing I am certain of: this joy cannot be given by any human being or any worldly object. It offers more hope each day than is possible to expe-

## 10. FROM BEING LOST TO BEING FOUND

rience in the flesh here on Earth, and it promises even greater fulfillment when we find ourselves in His presence.

After enduring what felt like an eternity of electric shocks, I realized that this is how we often feel when we face complications in life that seem endless and from which we can't find a way out. However, it's essential to remember that it is precisely during those difficult times that a wonderful light can suddenly appear, illuminating everything and making our pain disappear, no matter how intense it may be. God has the power and glory to alleviate our suffering and neutralize any remnants it may leave behind.

The struggles I went through prepared me to see clearly the great light that would come into my life. Now, I understand the scriptures that say the joy we can experience in this earthly existence pales in comparison to the joy we will have when we stand in the presence of the Lord. The intense emotions I still feel today as I reflect on that period make my eyes well up with tears and my emotions overflow. I can vividly relive those moments, and I know that it is by His grace that I can share this with you, dear reader.

As a mere human, I am aware of the flaws of this earthly life, and I sometimes feel ashamed to recount all that God has done for me and how merciful He has been because I don't believe I truly deserve all that He has given me. I have failed Him so many times and am very imperfect, with a strong and rebellious character. I have disobeyed repeatedly, and I accept painfully that I forgot Him. Yet, God never forgot me; He always remembered me and showed me mercy because He has a much larger plan than I ever imagined while I was searching in vain for "perfect plans" to achieve a happy life.

## RETURN HOME

Now I sense that God could say to me, "Leave behind those plans that only sink you deeper day after day. Stop searching unnecessarily and let me show you the path you must follow." This is how God acted in my life. It saddens me to know that thousands of people do not understand His call, but He is always present. I now comprehend everything because I was stubborn and foolish, believing only in my own thoughts and never considering other perspectives. I thought I was right in everything, but what I assumed often turned out to be the opposite. Before more tragic situations unfolded, He intervened and revealed the light to me.

He was always there, shepherding His lost sheep, waiting for them to return to the right path, and I was one of them. Despite my reluctance to understand, I moved further away and had to experience brokenness to find my way back Home. This experience showed me how merciful and great God truly is. Now, I can say, "I am finally back Home, Lord, so that You may do Your will with me."

Let me share with you a profound experience that changed my life. I often reflect on that moment, and I still can't fully grasp how the electric waves coursed through my body or how long the visions of light surrounded me. The peculiar thing is that, at the time, I didn't have a moment to contemplate why it happened to me or what message it contained. My mind seemed to transcend time; I had no memory of my present, no recollection of my past, and no reasoning for my future. It felt as if I was in another dimension.

And you know what, my dear friend who is reading this? Even if you don't feel close to God, after that experience, I don't remember

## 10. FROM BEING LOST TO BEING FOUND

how I got out of bed. I only recall being on the floor, getting onto my knees. I hadn't bent my knees like that in years and was at a loss for words. I lay in silence and sensed that God didn't require much from me at that moment; I was merely witnessing my own vulnerability—my strength, pride, and ego bending. There I was, kneeling, wholly humbled in His presence.

In Hebrew, the word for kneel is "Barak," which is related to the word "Berek," meaning knee. I believe the Hebrews saw the knees as a symbol of strength. Thus, bending my knees represented bowing my strength before the living God, recognizing that everything I am comes from Him. This act was crucial to understanding that God encouraged me to "take strength and prepare myself."

I don't remember conversing with God, and I would be lying if I said I did. I was kneeling there, silently offering myself to Him: "Here I am, surrendered at Your feet. I am all Yours; I have nothing, and I know nothing. This is new to me—do with me as You will." It felt as though I was confessing that I had pursued my paths and was now seeking His guidance on which direction to take. At that moment, I felt like I was beginning to live like I had just arrived and needed to learn to walk, talk, and connect with others.

Even though I couldn't fully express myself or comprehend what had just happened, I found myself whispering, "In the name of Jesus Christ... in the name of Jesus Christ... in the name of Jesus Christ..." After that, I rose from the floor and left the room. As I walked away, I kept repeating, "In Your name, in Your name, in Your name..." I went to the living room and sat in an armchair with large windows offering a beautiful view of the sky and trees, creating a forest-like ambiance. I sat there for a while, absorbing the breathtaking scenery and feeling entirely transformed.

Afterward, I moved to the kitchen, which also features large windows with a stunning view. I strolled, carefully observing everything around me, amazed by this newfound life. I even prepared a hot cup of tea before starting my daily activities. I must confess that from that morning on, my life changed utterly; nothing remained the same.

As I resumed my daily tasks, I struggled to interact with people. I preferred being alone and found it difficult to relate to others. I strolled as if I were rediscovering everything, analyzing my surroundings at a different pace. Everything appeared new, and I felt a tremendous weight within me that I could hardly manage. I longed to shout to the world about what I had seen and felt, but I couldn't find the words to express it; they just wouldn't come.

I found myself looking people in the eye as if I wanted to tell them, "I have something significant to reveal to you," but I stayed quiet. At the same time, I felt I had a lot to share, yet I worried they would think I was crazy or strange, so I held back for fear of rejection, of not expressing myself well, or that they wouldn't understand what I wanted to convey.

Maybe I might sound a little strange, but I am not mentally ill. I am entirely sure that the spirit of God came to me; therefore, I will no longer remain silent. I will share to the world that in these times, we are surrounded by lies and idolatry, and we often do not realize it. We live in the last times, and Jesus Christ is waiting for you with open arms to receive you when you return Home to make His glory shine in your life, Home, and family.

## 10. FROM BEING LOST TO BEING FOUND

I want to share something that I believe contains a secret message: In March 2023, I still cannot explain all the facts and details of those moments. I only know that God, with His infinite wisdom, manifested Himself in my life at the precise moment because He is never late for a crucial appointment but arrives just in time to bring glory to His name.

That day was unique; it had started calmly, almost typically. I was quiet and acting a little slow, unlike how I was used to being. I arrived Home after work around six in the evening, changed my clothes to relax, and unconsciously began collecting some jewelry I had in sight and used to wear daily. I also gathered some that I had stored in boxes, which I often combined for my daily outfits. Those who knew me through social media or my circle of friends understands what I mean: I usually wore one or more chains around my neck, beautiful bracelets on my wrists, and various rings and earrings.

All the jewelry I owned was made of 18 to 24-karat gold from the Middle East. They were beautiful, magnificent, and unique to the human eye. Later, I realized that I was organizing and separating the jewelry, but I had no idea why I was doing it. At no time during the day did I think about my valuable belongings or whether I should wear them. That day, when I arrived Home slowly, I decided to gather all these pieces quickly, regardless of their size, and ultimately, I placed them in a safe location, never to look at or use them again.

I never considered why I acted this way that day; I wanted to believe that God was clearing out everything in my life that was hindering me. Since then, He has been directing my steps. I remember repeating the same process with my makeup and wardrobe a few days later. However, let me clarify: I am not here to tell you that you should abandon all your belongings, nor am I judging you if you are different from me. I will respect and love you just the same. I want to share my life experiences from the past few years, what I have lived through, and how I have felt.

On the other hand, I want to sincerely thank you for reading my story. If I may ask you one thing, it is to keep the door open to what God can do in your life. He wants to perform miracles in your existence because you are unique to Him. Please do not dismiss what could be your greatest calling. Often, we close ourselves off when we refuse to listen to His voice. God wants to guide you out of darkness and into His marvelous light.

We should dare to leave behind what is commonplace in the world, the easy paths our society offers—those paths where we often avoid striving for anything meaningful or accepting the truth. It is disheartening, but today, we tend to cling to things that lack substance, to words not grounded in the Word of God.

When we do read it, we often only seek to understand what pleases our human sensibilities—what makes us feel good. Yet, when the text requires deep reflection, we might say, "The Word of God is not relevant for these times!" We claim that this era is different, that the teachings of the old are merely historical artifacts. This is not true! Jesus Christ never changes; He is the same yesterday, today, and forever. I encourage you to disregard empty phrases detached from the actual Word. The Word of God remains constant, even as humanity twists it to suit its desires.

## 10. FROM BEING LOST TO BEING FOUND

I understand that the world often shuns what is different. It prefers that we conform to the crowd, taking the broad path that is easier to walk. However, this wide path leads to earthly temptations and material luxuries, where we can quickly lose ourselves. Only the narrow path offers a great reward, but we must recognize that choosing this path will lead us to an immense, supernatural calling, far removed from the world of possessions and illusions. The path of God is spiritual, and His rewards are divine.

Following my supernatural and transformative experience, I have encountered other challenges that can be difficult for the human mind to comprehend. Some of these experiences may be hard for you to understand, or even raise doubts about their power. I can tell you that each person has their own path and calling. I ask that you remain open to what could save your life and not deny yourself a truth that may contain everything you have been seeking for years. Do not overlook the moment when the message you have awaited arrives, like a lightning bolt, to free you from all your ties.

I wish I could find the right words to express God's immense calling for me—not human words, but divine, angelic words that would allow my lips to move and articulate them. My greatest wish is that one day, you may experience that profound encounter that can completely transform your life.

With great humility, I confess that my days are different now. I want to reiterate that I am not an example for anyone. Under God's protection, I remind myself daily: "God the Father, I am not worthy to share everything you have revealed to me. I only thank you for the great mercy you have shown in my life—for raising me from the dead.

I was dead, and you brought me back to the light so that I could see. Just as you, merciful Father, resurrected Lazarus and called him from his tomb, saying, 'Lazarus, come forth,' you told me to 'Rise' from the dead because I was dead in life. I was blind, and now I can see."

If you wish, and if you are reading this right now, know that He says to you, "Get up," and He will light your path. A blessing is coming to your life, Home, or family—receive it and move forward. This happened in my life; God lifted me from the darkness to show me His light, which He wants to do for you. Don't deny yourself the great blessing that awaits you.

I must tell you that you should ignore the criticism you may receive if you choose to accept this calling. Those who were once close to you may question your decisions, and you may end up feeling alone. You might find that you no longer fit in with your old circle of friends, but this is not bad; it's part of the journey. I'm not suggesting you isolate yourself; I would never advocate for that. Instead, understand that change is a natural part of life, and you will need to make space for the blessings that God wants to bring into your life. Trust that these will be great things.

Soon, you will discover that those who follow God are meant to share the message. This powerful word should not be hidden because it represents the light for those who walk in darkness. This divine message will impact many people; your life will no longer have limits. The world will not define your boundaries; you no longer belong to it as you once did. Now, you are with God— the great, merciful God who creates paths where none seem to exist and performs miracles that only you can feel and witness.

## 10. FROM BEING LOST TO BEING FOUND

Recognize the Guardian of the promise who reassured you: "I will not abandon you or leave you; I will be here taking care of you all the days of your life." You will see that God is a powerful counselor. All you need to do is get on your knees and talk to Him; you'll feel His listening presence, and He will take on your burdens. He is the Almighty, the breaker of chains, our great Savior, our light, and our path. I could use countless names to describe Him, for He encompasses everything.

You might be thinking to yourself, "What a wonderful experience!" And indeed, it is a tremendous blessing. However, remember that "from Eve" one to whom much has been given, much will be required, and from the one to whom much has been entrusted, even more will be asked." I am fully aware of this responsibility and reflect on it every day. Knowing His great power and promises also brings you that responsibility.

There is no more extended room for the trivial concerns of this world. I must now be cautious with the words I write, and every day, I pray for God to enlighten me and guide me as He sees fit. I ask Him to bless me and help me see the vision He has prepared for me, to open my ears so I can hear His voice and obey Him, and to help me be mindful of every word that comes out of my mouth and every step I take. I seek His wisdom to ensure that my words and actions align with His will.

I must tell you that you should ignore the criticism you may receive if you choose to accept this calling. Those who were once close to you may question your decisions, and you may end up feeling alone. You might find that you no longer fit in with your old circle of friends, but this is not bad; it's part of the journey. I'm not suggesting you isolate yourself; I would never advocate for that. Instead, understand that change is a natural part of life, and you will need to make space for the blessings that God wants to bring into your life. Trust that these will be great things.

Soon, you will discover that those who follow God are meant to share the message. This powerful word should not be hidden because it represents the light for those who walk in darkness. This divine message will impact many people; your life will no longer have limits. The world will not define your boundaries; you no longer belong to it as you once did. Now, you are with God— the great, merciful God who creates paths where none seem to exist and performs miracles that only you can feel and witness.

Recognize the Guardian of the promise who reassured you: "I will not abandon you or leave you; I will be here taking care of you all the days of your life." You will see that God is a powerful counselor. All you need to do is get on your knees and talk to Him; you'll feel His listening presence, and He will take on your burdens. He is the Almighty, the breaker of chains, our great Savior, our light, and our path. I could use countless names to describe Him, for He encompasses everything.

You might be thinking to yourself, "What a wonderful experience!" And indeed, it is a tremendous blessing. However, remember that "from Eve" one to whom much has been given, much will be required, and from the one to whom much has been entrusted, even more will be asked." I am fully aware of this responsibility and reflect on it every day. Knowing His great power and promises also brings you that responsibility.

## 10. FROM BEING LOST TO BEING FOUND

There is no more extended room for the trivial concerns of this world. I must now be cautious with the words I write, and every day, I pray for God to enlighten me and guide me as He sees fit. I ask Him to bless me and help me see the vision He has prepared for me, to open my ears so I can hear His voice and obey Him, and to help me be mindful of every word that comes out of my mouth and every step I take. I seek His wisdom to ensure that my words and actions align with His will.

God has not called me back Home to be paralyzed or to hide my light. He has called me to be on a lamp stand, shining brightly alongside others who have also returned Home. We need to pay attention to the signs, as this is the way we can receive God's Mercy. Only then will His infinite light, which fills everything with glory, be able to manifest in us.

# 11

# Beyond reconciliation

Aware of God's greatness, I experience a daily return Home, heeding His signs and wonders after many years of challenging circumstances, failures, and navigating dark valleys.

How does the return Home happen? There is something extraordinary about the concept of returning. For instance, when we have visitors in our Homes who are about to leave, we sincerely say, "Thank you very much for coming. I hope you revisit us soon." As a businesswoman, I enjoy saying, "Please come back soon."

I have owned a furniture store for several years, and when a customer enters, I first like to say "Welcome." We treat our customers joyfully and strive to make them feel comfortable. After they have spent much time looking at and experiencing the furniture, we say, "Thank you for coming. I hope you come back soon" as they leave.

If they return to the store, the same staff or whoever is present will greet them warmly, saying, "Welcome back! It's so nice to see you." The service becomes closer and friendlier, fostering a sense of trust. We might say, "Look, sit here, make yourself comfortable.

Can I get you some tea? Would you like a glass of water? How have you been?" This approach makes the conversation more relaxed and enjoyable, creating a Homely atmosphere.

Now, I want to discuss another context of "return." This return comes after enduring a life filled with disasters, difficulties, illnesses, disappointments, and discouragement. It reflects the experience of wandering through dark valleys, feeling as if we are dead in life, and facing hunger—not just for food, but for spiritual fulfillment. It is a return from a period of being lost, struggling to find a way out of an extended season in the darkest desert.

When we find ourselves in the saddest conditions of our lives, devoid of peace or purpose because we lack direction, we can feel disconnected from our true identity. We miss the light that can help us regain our calm and joy, that sense of having enough even in the face of unmet human needs. However, when we find that peace, it becomes clear that it is sufficient for survival.

Our heavenly Father's greatest joy is seeing us return to Him after enduring struggles along our paths. This reminds me of the parable of the prodigal son. In this story, a father has two sons. The younger son requests his inheritance, and the father, without hesitation, grants his wish. The younger son then goes far away and squanders all his possessions, getting lost in the world's temptations.

As you grow up and seek to explore the world, you may feel the urge to do things your way and impose your ideas. You might believe that you have the strength to forge ahead, and you may ask God for "your inheritance" to pursue your ambitions. However, you will likely encounter many challenges along the way—illness, hunger,

## 11. BEYOND RECONCILIATION

and possibly even the loss of everything, much like the younger son in the parable.

He ultimately found no way out except to return to his father's house, seeking forgiveness and asking to be accepted, even as one of his father's hired servants. Yet, his father did not reject him. Instead, he welcomed him back with open arms, saying to his servants: "Bring out the best robe and put it on him, and put a ring on his hand and shoes on his feet. And bring the fatted calf and kill it, and let us eat and celebrate, for this my son was dead and is alive again; he was lost and is found." (Luke 15:22-24, NKJV).

How many of us would long for such a warm welcome after hitting rock bottom and enduring complicated experiences during dark times? God rejoices when we return to Him, recognizing that, after wasting our lives, we can find comfort in His presence.

If we decide to return, there is a grand celebration in the house of the Lord, and we are ushered into new horizons and spiritual dimensions we might never have imagined. Indeed, there is immense joy and celebration when we turn away from a lost life filled with hunger, fatigue, and uncertainty, as illustrated in the parable of the prodigal son. If you find yourself in such circumstances, dear reader, I ask you: why not return? God delights in rejoicing and celebrating the return of each of us to His House.

This is how we are reunited with the Creator—how our Father welcomes us after we make mistakes and squander His inheritance, the wonderful inheritance of His word. It is akin to the parable of the prodigal son: God sees us from afar, approaching defeated and in pain. He sees us helpless, full of bitterness, and even dirty.

Yet, despite this, He welcomes us with open arms. He never reproaches us or asks why we left or how we wasted everything. He does not ask what we need now that we have returned. No reproaches; instead, He welcomes us with a great celebration, asking that the best clothes be brought for us and preparing the most extravagant banquets because we were lost and have now returned Home. In my reunion with God, after being lost for a long time, I experienced a glorious welcome.

I did not know what would come next, but I humbly thanked Him for that moment and for the new, amazing experiences that were unfolding. Never doubt God, even if your current state is lamentable; He is working silently for you. He acts quietly to give you a purpose and wants to create a masterpiece with you. Therefore, you must distance yourself from the noise of the world—the superficial distractions that surround us—so that you can hear His call. Stop listening to the noise of the world. Avoid reading empty books filled with hollow philosophies, and refrain from watching television programs that do not nourish your spirit. Remember, the enemy uses many distractions to separate you from God.

It is important to withdraw from toxic people and those who claim to offer spiritual peace in exchange for money. Be cautious of those who tell you that you do not need to go to church to be close to God, that He does not mind if you attend congregations or His House as long as you have faith. I insist: do not forget that the enemy's sole purpose is to destroy you, to lead you away from your Father's house and His ways. He sets traps, insisting that to be holy and please God, it is unnecessary to seek Him in church.

## 11. BEYOND RECONCILIATION

As we've already mentioned, you will need to leave the wide path that leads many to destruction and choose the narrow path if you truly desire something supernatural to manifest in your life. The wide path is easy to walk; it requires little contemplation of your options, as everything is laid out by others' footsteps. Although it is a broad path, it is also where it is easiest to fall into superficiality, doing things out of habit. This path is filled with empty trends in style, consumption, and living, where you are guided without thought about where to go, how to behave, what to do, and even how to live with your family because "that world" offers everything on a silver platter.

It may seem incredible, but everything is presented to us through various means. We see it on television, where we are offered the best experiences to live. On social networks, we encounter advice that is often full of pretense, alongside life coaches promising emotional and physical stability while using manipulative tactics. There are also spiritual gurus who claim to help us discover our so-called higher self, but in reality, they only seek power, money, and material wealth. They ensnare us with their misleading messages. This notion of a higher self is misleading because it conveys that without it, we are nothing and can achieve nothing.

Many of these spiritual teachers even use biblical lessons to grab our attention, promoting prosperity gospels that encourage us to follow our own desires rather than what God truly wants for us. I, too, fell into these deceptions and traps. I believed in false promises and distanced myself from God. I then had to struggle against all odds to cultivate a genuine and deep relationship with Him. I used to think that the day of my death and awakening to a new life, that day filled with immense light, would mark the end of my existence.

Little did I know that this moment would signal the beginning of new beginnings and new horizons, filled with messages and experiences. I am still on a journey to understand what God has been revealing to me daily through signs, which continue to emerge and show me just a glimpse of His greatness and power. In light of this, all I can do is yield and allow Him to grant me understanding, recognizing that our human minds are often limited in grasping the incredible nature of God's ways and His methods of teaching us about the celestial essence.

Everything is presented through words, symbols, and moments—one after another, signs and more signs. If I don't share every detail with you, it is not out of a desire to hide anything. Sometimes, even I struggle to interpret these signs, but I feel and see them. I ask you to take away only what you can understand, without forcing any interpretation. Remember that God uses different stages and times to unfold His plan for us, and through His messages, He reveals His wonderful way of making His glory known to us.

We must recognize that, as human beings, we do not have the mental capacity to fully comprehend all of His wonders and wisdom at once. However, we should not doubt that His glory will reveal itself, and everything will come to light in due time. There is no need to despair; "To everything there is a season, and a time for every purpose under heaven" (Ecclesiastes 3:3, NKJV). We should always be attentive to the ways God communicates with us and be aware when He requires something from us.

## 11. BEYOND RECONCILIATION

When you feel like you don't understand anything, don't deny it. You might eventually find the information that clarifies things for you and solves what seems puzzling or strange to others. The truth is that something significant is about to happen. Trust that God will do what He needs to do in your life.

Don't question everything or deny what you don't know or fully understand yet. That's how God works—often in ways that we, as humans, cannot comprehend. Everything will come to us in due time, so don't doubt it; God's timing is perfect.

Now I'd like to share something that was hard for me to grasp, which demonstrates that God's signs come in stages and times. One day, a word came to my mind: "Come down." It appeared suddenly, without a clear reason at that moment. It wasn't a word I frequently used, so I surprised myself by saying, "Hilda, come down…" and I thought, "But where?" This word troubled me, and despite searching for its meaning, I couldn't find its origin.

On another occasion, early one morning, around five o'clock, I was awakened by a voice repeating, "Get up, get up, get up…" I didn't feel fear, as I had experienced similar calls before. I reflected deeply on that voice, but ultimately did not get up.

The next night, it was not a voice but a loud buzzing in my ears that woke me. It was an unfamiliar sensation. I got up to see what was happening, thinking that acting quickly would help me interpret the signal and understand the message. However, that wasn't the case, so I returned to bed and fell asleep.

Remember: stage by stage and time by time. When you have returned to the House of the Lord, do not fear or be dismayed. Don't ask too many questions; accept the call with faith. Do not worry. Even if the narrow path is more difficult, listen to the word of God and move forward. We sometimes stray from our paths because they are complicated, and we seek easier routes, but they only lead us into darkness. Always remember: you must not mix darkness with light; the paths of darkness and light do not intertwine.

Listen for the voice that will someday tell you: "Leave your country and your relatives and come to the land that I will show you." These words hold the key to something you alone must do. This precious call is meant for you, and God has been preparing your way. Try not to walk alongside those who dwell in darkness; your path is different and unique.

Do not fear God's word or what He asks of you. What I'm sharing today isn't something I read in a book; it's something I lived through. That's why I can tell you that your call is a personal gift from God. It's your inheritance, and He wants you to share His wonders and the transformations He has made in your life, so that His name may be glorified.

When you return Home—whether after walking through darkness, seeking a place to dwell, or feeling spiritually disconnected while your physical body is at Home—it's important to understand that you cannot divide yourself to be with God. You cannot have one foot in and one foot out. We are either fully present or we are not. It should not resemble some marriages that have existed together for years yet remain emotionally distant. Only by being fully together and attentive can we truly hear God's call and experience the wonderful things that await us.

## 11. BEYOND RECONCILIATION

When you are on the path that God has for you, you don't need to worry about how to start talking to Him or what to say—or even what not to say. He is all-powerful and knows everything. He molds us like a skilled potter, and we are the clay in His hands. Let Him enter your life! I remember one morning, around five o'clock, I felt what I can only describe as a great wave of wind on the right side of my body. That sensation woke me up and spoke to my spirit. I felt an overwhelming need to move my lips and exclaim, "Holy, holy, holy." It was a wonderful moment—one that filled me with incredible joy. My lips uttered those words effortlessly, and I felt as though that was the only thing I could say to God at that moment.

No other words came to mind; I simply recited that praise because it flowed from my heart—"holy, holy, holy." I, an imperfect human, was deeply moved that God placed those words on my lips to honor His glory and to praise His merciful name: the King who was, is, and is to come. I don't know what challenges you have faced in your life or the wonders God has worked in you, but I am certain that many of us have great stories of miracles and blessings to share.

At this moment, the story of the demoniac of Gadara comes to mind, found in the Gospel of Saint Luke, chapter 8, verses 26-39 (NKJV). In this passage, Jesus and His disciples arrived in the region of the Gadarenes, on the other side of the Sea of Galilee. There, a man possessed by demons came out to meet them from the tombs. He was in a pitiful condition, living naked among the tombs, isolated from society. He was so violent that no one could control him. The demons had tormented him for a long time, and he often broke the chains that people used to try to bind him.

# RETURN HOME

When the man saw Jesus, he cried out and fell on his knees before Him, saying, "What have you to do with me, Jesus, Son of the Most High God? I beg You, do not torment me." Jesus asked him his name, and he replied, "Legion," because many demons had entered him.

The demons begged Jesus not to send them into the abyss, but to let them enter a herd of pigs that was nearby. Jesus let them do so, and the demons came out of the man and entered the pigs. The herd rushed down a cliff and drowned in the lake.

After this, the people of the area came to see what had happened. They found the man who had previously been possessed sitting at Jesus' feet, clothed and in his right mind. This sight filled them with great fear. Those who had witnessed the events shared what Jesus had done, leading the people of the region to ask Jesus to leave, as they were overwhelmed with fear. The man who had been freed from the demons begged Jesus to allow him to accompany Him. However, Jesus told him to return Home and share everything that God had done for him.

The man obeyed and began to spread the news throughout the city, proclaiming how Jesus had freed him. Just as you have reconciled with God and experienced the miracles and wonders He has brought into your life, He also desires something from you at this moment: He wants you to share the wonderful works He has done in your life. "Go Home and tell how great things God has done for you." So he went away, proclaiming throughout the entire city how much Jesus had done for him. Luke 8:39 (NKJV).

# 12

# Visions of the return: revelations along the way

Life is filled with symbols and signs that God places on our paths to awaken us, inspire us, and elevate us to new dimensions. However, no matter how many warnings He sends, how many trains pass before us, or how loud the noise might be, we often resist waking from the deep slumber we find ourselves in.

We may fail to understand these calls and remain unaware that we are merely passengers in this life. It's crucial to pay attention to every opportunity that presents itself. Consider this: will you continue in your deep sleep without taking action to make your life a masterpiece in the hands of the Lord? There is no time to waste! "The night is far gone, and the day is at hand…"

For many years, I struggled to understand the signs that God sent me. The darkness enveloping me was so profound that I couldn't discern the path I needed to take. My vision was limited, and I was unable to see what was about to enter my life. "Without prophecy, the people are unrestrained; but he who keeps the law is blessed." When we lack a clear vision of where we are and where we are going, the journey of self-discovery becomes difficult and dark.

Our lives lose meaning, leading us to choices that sink us deeper into despair, making the return to our true selves even longer. I found myself trapped in this abyss. The enemy kept me immersed in worldly distractions, leaving me stuck and lacking vision. Every time I tried to move forward, I felt pulled two steps back. I couldn't experience peace or find my way out of this desert.

God had to take my hand and pull me from the emotional and physical breakdowns that were driving me back to the light of His presence. It was not an easy journey. As I have shared before, I endured many sleepless nights, struggling to find rest and inner peace. I turned to doctors, medications, relaxing herbs, and any remedy I could think of to regain that lost peace and fall asleep again. But God did not want me to sleep—at least not yet. He wanted me awake and alert to grasp what He was trying to show me. Even when I screamed, "Why me?" His voice whispered back, "If you truly want your life to be restored and transformed, I must break you and mold you in My way, not yours."

At times, I felt as though my body had no breath left. During the day, I was drained of energy, and as night fell, I felt the anguish of being unable to close my eyes and sleep. My body no longer felt like my own; I was motionless and exhausted. Until one day, I finally surrendered. I closed my eyes and said, "Lord, I have no strength left. I've tried to rest and can't. Now, please take control of my life and do with me as You will."

Suddenly, I fell into a deep sleep and began to have visions. Messages written in Hebrew, a language I didn't understand, were

## 12. VISIONS OF THE RETURN: REVELATIONS ALONG THE WAY

revealed to me. I had never seen Hebrew before, yet I instinctively knew that these messages were meant for me; they were something that God destined for my understanding. When I finally woke up, I realized that if He had sent me these signs, it was for a very important reason.

The next night, I focused on understanding the revelations that came to me through dreams. I felt uncertain but also a great responsibility. I wanted to absorb everything being presented to me and didn't want to miss a single detail. Suddenly, I was transported back to my childhood. I saw myself sitting at a desk, paying attention to every word that came from the teacher's mouth, preparing for the most important exam of my life.

I wanted to take out a pen and write everything down, to record in my mind every symbol, every letter, and every essence of the message. The nerves and responsibility were overwhelming. My nights became profound lessons for life. As soon as it got dark, I prepared myself to receive those divine lessons—those nighttime classes that gave new meaning to my mission in this world. Although my outer life seemed normal, my inner world was like a puzzle that God was assembling, piece by piece.

He was taking all those broken fragments and putting them back together, forming a masterpiece, because that is how He works: He rebuilds us. On another night, I was ready to sleep again, eager to learn. I quietly climbed under the covers, lay down, and closed my eyes. This time, the message came in Latin. At 5:00 in the morning, the visions began to unfold. I could understand a bit more, perhaps God thought, "I will make it easier for you," knowing how stubborn and hard of hearing we can be when He asks something of us. I clearly remember this vision: letters and numbers flowed from one side to the other, merging into vertical and horizontal lines. I struggled with all my strength to put them in order.

Everything was spinning, rising, and falling, like a massive screen filled with codes that had never before been reproduced. What was being presented to me transcended our worldly understanding; it was something celestial—something that the human mind cannot fully grasp.

This is what His Word says: "But the natural man does not receive the things of the Spirit of God, for they are foolishness to him; neither can he know them, because they are spiritually discerned" (1 Corinthians 2:14, NKJV). As we have seen, these truths can seem foolish to us. We live in a world of unbelief, where the wonders from above can only be understood on a spiritual level. To grasp and believe in God's truths, we must continually strive to reach higher spiritual levels. Recently, I experienced a new revelation early one morning. I realized that as time goes on, the visions I receive become increasingly complex and difficult to understand. This is the nature of God's wonders. Sometimes, we may not fully comprehend them, and that's okay. We should simply receive them as they come. In due time, God will grant us the wisdom to understand His will according to His revelations. So, do not give up on what you can't understand right now; everything will be revealed in its proper time.

During this revelation, I saw an ancient scroll passing before me, moving slowly from left to right. The scroll was very old, with faded edges as if weathered by time. It contained messages written in

## 12. VISIONS OF THE RETURN: REVELATIONS ALONG THE WAY

Hebrew on a sheet of ancient papyrus. Gradually, I began to understand more of what was written; the language became familiar to me. At that moment, I stopped trying to interpret what I saw and turned my eyes toward God. I asked Him to manifest Himself in my life and to use me as an instrument for His purposes. I sought His forgiveness for being distant from Him for so many years, while also expressing my gratitude for what He was doing in my life.

I placed my life entirely in His hands, trusting in His plans for me. I have faith in His Holy Name because in Him there is power. I have witnessed His great mercy working in supernatural ways. He presents wonderful scenes in our lives as if they were taken from a great movie. This is how God is—trust in Him! He has something magnificent prepared for you. These are not just motivational words like those found in some self-help books that claim everything will be okay. I share this from my heart because I have experienced it firsthand, and I still feel His presence as I write these words.

If you live your life without sensing His presence, perhaps you are lost in the distractions of the earthly world. I have known His miracles because He transformed my life in an instant. His love for me was so immense that He had to break my tendons, bones, and nerves to awaken me and pull me out of the darkness where I felt dead, without hope of seeing His glorious light.

The most beautiful part is that He wants to show you those wonders too, and I am not the only one chosen. Right now, He desires to bring you out of the dark valley you find yourself in and reveal what He can do for your life, your Home, and your family. HOW GLORIOUS IT IS! His glory is so remarkable that, on that night,

He had no hesitation in showing me the way through that papyrus written in Hebrew.

It was a very old text, light brown, its original hue almost faded, with pieces missing from the corners, yet the written message remained intact. Dear reader, you may not know much about the powerful God named Jesus Christ. Perhaps you have heard of His miracles, but you might think that such events do not exist today or will never happen to you. If you have distanced yourself from Him, I invite you now to return to God and to His promises, which never fail.

If you return to Him, everything will pass. If you return Home, your life will change because you will no longer live in unknown lands; you will live under His promise, and one day we will see Him face to face, just as He is: pure splendor!

That morning, these thoughts flowed slowly through my mind. The vision became clear and traversed every part of my consciousness. I felt calm, yet I tried hard to grasp each message written on that papyrus in Hebrew. Although I couldn't understand it completely, I could decipher that His word is faithful and true. It is not just a historical fact; it is a present reality. Through Him, great things are about to come, and surprising events are imminent.

"Search the Scriptures, for you think that in them, you will have eternal life; and they are the ones that bear witness of me" (John 5:39). Thus, we must return to the past, to antiquities, and to the depths of the Scriptures to understand the divine message and inherit its promise: eternal life.

On another one of those wonderful early mornings, just as the Hebrew text came to me, a vision unfolded from left to right in my

## 12. VISIONS OF THE RETURN: REVELATIONS ALONG THE WAY

mind. I saw a beautiful face, round and fair-skinned, with wavy gray hair reaching his shoulders. His thick beard matched his hair, about four inches long. His large, beautiful eyes radiated a glow that illuminated everything around him. With his mouth closed, and his gaze fixed on me, he passed through my mind like a stunning portrait, flooding me with his presence. Oh, you are holy! Only you can show us your glory.

Not all the visions were peaceful; some were quite turbulent, like the one I am about to describe. I felt an overwhelming force in my body and struggled not to look at what was being revealed to me, but the power of God is greater than that of any human. That morning, something struck me hard on the forehead and pulled me deep into a very high mountain. Everything happened so fast, like a flash of lightning; just as it took me to that mountain, it brought me back to my bed. It was an indescribable force that held me back and wouldn't let me go. In that moment, I felt afraid and very small before that magnificent mountain. "What is man that you are mindful of him, and the son of man, that you visit him?" (Psalm 8:4-5, NKJV). Oh, poor me! A simple human being overwhelmed with fear at the sight of what was being shown to me. Yet God, in His great mercy, did not regard my faults or my resistance to receiving His message; He only sought to show me His wonders.

His strength is so immense that it overwhelms us. That night, I felt how he oppressed me repeatedly. He transported me to that mountain and brought me back to the earthly plane like a whip that comes and goes with great speed and impact.

Once I stopped resisting and accepted his presence, I allowed him to guide me in his way. He took me to the peak of that enormous and fabulous mountain. From the top, I saw a great city at my feet, full of lights and fully illuminated. It was one of the most beautiful sights I have ever witnessed in my life. Its glow was breathtaking, and a profound silence enveloped the scene.

I don't know about you, but I do want to be in that great city; I want to be part of the grand celebration there. What do you think? Are you ready? Get prepared! Fight the good fight so that no one takes your place. We will see each other there. When they call the roll, I want to shout, "Present!" When you look at the color red, what emotions does it evoke in you? What do you associate it with? Perhaps fire, danger, love, passion, or even blood. It is indeed a striking color, yet I had not given it much thought until that morning...

That day, I woke up feeling uneasy. The visions I had experienced were displayed to me in bright red letters—intense and overwhelming. They moved from top to bottom and left to right. I don't think they formed a specific word; they simply drifted around, and no matter how hard I tried to arrange them into a coherent message, I couldn't. I got up to go to the bathroom, my heart racing, and even though I was awake, the red letters continued to surround me. A few nights later, while I was sleeping soundly, a voice whispered to me, "Wake up, open your eyes." I looked up at the ceiling and saw everything glowing in a brilliant red. I stared at it for a few moments before closing my eyes again and drifting back to sleep. That's when I knew it was time.

# 13

# Living water to quench spiritual thirst

"Whoever drinks of this water will thirst again, but whoever drinks of the water I give him will never thirst, but the water I give him will become in him a spring of water welling up to eternal life" (John 4:13-14).

When I began my search to satisfy the spiritual hunger I felt in 2000, I knew there was a better way to live amidst the emptiness in my life. I was aware that there was much more to discover, and that the experiences I had and the path I had taken did not compare to what God had planned for me.

I understood that the pain would not disappear immediately, but I knew I had to move forward in my search for God. Dear friends and brothers who are reading these lines, in those moments, we can place our hands on our hearts and say: "Grace taught my soul to pray and made my eyes shed tears; it is grace that has always kept me and will never abandon me." He finds us and satisfies our hunger and thirst for justice with the divine gift of His grace—not because we deserve it, but because He loves us unconditionally.

Even when we turn away, He works in our lives and comforts our souls. I wanted to fill that hunger and void more than I feared the unknown. I was willing to do anything, no matter the cost. I didn't care if I died on the way to discovering how to escape the bitterness of my life. I didn't want to leave this world without experiencing joy and security. I yearned to soar into new dimensions. It felt like a gamble—with everything to lose or gain. As the poet Erin Hanson said, "What if I fall? Oh, but baby, what if you fly?" This sentiment perfectly captured my situation and motivated me, giving me the energy and enthusiasm to continue on my journey. I now realize that my greatest longing was to have a personal relationship with the great I AM.

During my search, I asked myself a series of questions: What is this void I'm trying to fill? What am I doing to address it? Where am I headed? What legacy will I leave behind? Who or what inspires me the most? What fears or insecurities are holding me back from fully utilizing the talents that God has given me to fulfill my purpose in life? What makes me feel fulfilled and happy? What do I enjoy sharing and experiencing with others? I spent a long time pondering these questions—sometimes with concern, other times with nostalgia, and sometimes feeling quite distant from the true calling that would bring me back Home. At that time, I didn't believe I needed to take action; I just wanted answers without discomfort, without stepping out of my comfort zone, and without seeking another path.

I thought that in that place I would receive answers to all the questions I had been asking myself. The truth is that those answers do not come when we remain stuck in our comfort zone. We need to allow ourselves to be guided and be prepared to take on responsibility

## 13. LIVING WATER TO QUENCH SPIRITUAL THIRST

and effort when required of us. Moreover, this journey involves obedience before we receive what we seek, as sometimes being obedient can cause discomfort.

Consider the parable of the prodigal son. What would have happened if he had not returned Home? He didn't spend much time contemplating his decision or doubting whether to go back: "What will my father say? Will he kick me out? What will my father's servants think?"

I imagine he didn't ask himself as many questions as we might think. He simply humbled himself, took action, and returned. To reach that point, he had to get out of his own way and choose obedience. That son didn't say, "My father has many assets; I'll ask him for more money to keep wasting." Instead, he likely thought, "Enough is enough." He couldn't bear to stay hungry when he knew that in his father's house, he could have everything, and they would welcome him back with joy. This illustrates what happens to us when we demand answers to our questions and want our requests to be heard. It's important to note that God doesn't demand our obedience just to put us at His feet. He is like the father in the story of the prodigal son.

When he sees his son in the distance, he doesn't wait for him to come crawling back. Similarly, our heavenly Father, in His goodness, quickly comes to meet us with joy once He sees us take action to return to Him. After experiencing spiritual hunger, we must be obedient and take steps toward our return Home. Only then will we find true satisfaction.

To quench this spiritual thirst for righteousness, we need to do more than just ask or question our circumstances. It requires a significant amount of obedience on our part, followed by a sense of responsibility. Taking responsibility often means making moves that feel uncomfortable; however, we may be reluctant to embrace these feelings because they involve actions that require effort and sacrifice. Feeling hungry and thirsty for righteousness is a very positive sign.

Despite the challenges and difficulties you might encounter along the way, if you're currently experiencing a sense of emptiness, you should feel hopeful. This spiritual hunger indicates that doors will eventually open for you, and that longing will be satisfied with rivers of living water. "Blessed are those who hunger and thirst for righteousness, for He satisfies the needy soul and fills the hungry soul with goodness" (Psalm 107:9, NKJV).

"It is good to have longings, and the more intense they are, the better. The Lord will satisfy the longings of the soul, no matter how great or absorbing they may be. Let us long greatly, for the Lord will satisfy us greatly. We shall never be in the right frame of mind if we are content with ourselves and free from longings.

Desires for greater grace, along with unutterable groans, are signs of growth, and we should desire them more and more. Blessed Spirit, lead us to sigh and cry for better things and to ask for more of the best! Hunger is not a pleasant sensation. Yet, blessed are those who hunger and thirst for righteousness.

Such individuals will find that their hunger is not appeased by mere scraps but will be satisfied. They will not settle for coarse food, but their diet will be worthy of the good Lord, and they will be nourished by what comes from Jehovah Himself.

Let us not be anxious because we long and hunger. Instead, let us listen to the voice of the Psalmist as he expresses his longing

## 13. LIVING WATER TO QUENCH SPIRITUAL THIRST

to see God exalted: "Let them give thanks to the Lord for his loving-kindness and his wonderful works to the sons of men." I spent a lot of time overwhelmed by many questions I asked God and myself. I reflected on them for hours, pondering possible answers. Some of these took me longer to resolve because I was unsure of my clarity; I didn't know if the answers were entirely sincere or fully addressed my concerns.

The only questions that were clear from the beginning were: What am I running away from? Now I understand that my greatest fear was in attending to my most significant calling, one that far surpasses any monetary gain or title I have achieved in my life. This calling cannot be compared to any financial reward. The other question was:

What must I do to feel truly fulfilled and happy? The answer is to fulfill my mission. This realization brings me joy, hope, and motivation because I now know what my true mission is; it has been revealed to me, and I am ready to follow this wonderful path alongside you. I would be very happy to have the opportunity to speak with you one day and to hear if you, too, have experienced deep darkness and have now stepped into the light. When I say that you should be very "hungry," it may sound ambitious, but we must be cautious about how we satisfy our spiritual hunger, as it can lead us down paths that are not aligned with God's Will."

I remember that when I began this search, I wrote extensively. From very early on, my mind became active, and I jotted down things that motivated me, capturing the desires of my heart on paper. Wherever I went—whether on a plane, on the road, or at Home—I carried my journal with me and began to write about my vision for my life and my great search.

It's funny how I wrote down so many desires, thoughts, reflections, and longings, all while not knowing exactly what I was looking for. Was I searching for myself? Was I searching for God? This is why I emphasize that to achieve what you want, you must have a tremendous spiritual hunger. You shouldn't settle for the little things, but instead reach out to the Almighty and ask Him to show you the way. He will respond; He will have mercy on you, just as He had mercy on me. "Call to me and I will answer you; I will show you great and hidden things that you do not know." – Jeremiah 33:3 (NKJV).

At the beginning of my search, I spent days sitting on the floor, crying for hours. I spoke to God and asked Him to guide me. I was tired of living an empty life. I asked Him to direct me to where I truly needed to be because I understood that my destiny was not tied to material possessions. I wasn't interested in luxuries. Prior to this journey of self-discovery (when I was spiritually blind—now I can see), I had enjoyed wonderful experiences, but they were always through a material lens—jewelry, travel, money. I was exhausted from that. What I needed was to lead a spiritually fulfilling life. I yearned to feel God's presence, to experience the supernatural, and to satisfy the hunger that lingered for so many years. I needed guidance to receive something far greater than fleeting desires. I don't know how you feel right now; I don't know how hungry you are to experience something extraordinary in your life—not in terms of material wealth or fame, but in elevating yourself to a spiritual level you've never felt before.

## 13. LIVING WATER TO QUENCH SPIRITUAL THIRST

Don't stop until you feel the presence of God. If I can share one thing, it's that experiencing His call is one of the most wonderful feelings you can have. Once He calls you to His presence, you dive deep into His Spirit. You begin to understand your path and what God wants from you; you think about how to please Him and serve Him with each moment. Your days change; every moment becomes a new opportunity to satisfy your spiritual hunger.

When you reach this point and look back, you realize that your life now has meaning, gradually filling that spiritual void. But be careful! Analyze your thoughts. I'm not asking you to share this with me; instead, reflect on it for yourself as you read this. Question whether what you are doing and living today aligns with the path that God has for you. Confess and have a serious conversation with Him because He will reveal everything to you in His time. Health experts advise us to be mindful of what we consume in excess, and this applies to our spiritual hunger as well.

Sometimes, in our eagerness to satisfy that hunger, we consume whatever is immediately available; but what fills us is not necessarily what nourishes the spirit. Occasionally, instead of food, we need something else—like water. We may be spiritually dehydrated and need to drink in God's mercy. That's why it's crucial that each step we take is guided toward Him and our true mission. You may be going through a stressful time, or something in your life may be making you feel empty.

The solution won't be found in material things. That hunger cannot be satisfied with jewelry, money, or luxury items. While you might feel a temporary sense of satisfaction, soon you'll find yourself hungry again. This hunger can only be satisfied with nourishment for your soul. You might also find yourself surrounded by people who don't contribute to your spiritual journey—individuals who have no interest in God or even in discussing the Bible (believe me, I was once one of them)—engaging in superficial and materialistic relationships.

Be cautious! Everything I share here comes from my own experiences; I'm not making anything up. There was a time when I surrounded myself with people who had nothing to do with my faith and my desire to understand the purpose that God had for me. A significant realization for me was understanding that some people in the same church were not willing to explore the depths of their spirituality; they were spiritually dormant, attending church as a mere Sunday habit. Therefore, evaluate your spiritual thermostat: determine how hungry you are to stay on this path and continue, now, with greater desire and strength. The more you strive, the more your life will evolve from victory to victory.

If you feel spiritually dead, as though you are no longer the person you once were or that you have never truly connected with God, it's time to wake up! Get up and take action. Don't stay silent; speak to the Lord. Say to Him, "Here I am in Your presence. I want to feel hungry for You and for Your presence. I want to understand Your word. Please uncover my ears so that I can hear Your voice and open my eyes to see the vision You have prepared for me. Ignite the fire of the Holy Spirit in my life."

If you sense that your spirit is numb and your mind no longer thinks clearly about God's will, ask yourself what you are doing as you sit in that state. I understand that uncertainty can cloud your vision,

## 13. LIVING WATER TO QUENCH SPIRITUAL THIRST

but don't simply sit with your arms crossed. Respond to God's call and seek Him—don't wait for Him to come to you.

Light the fire of faith within you. Become kindling for that flame so it can grow and spread, reaching new heights, making you a vessel for His honor. Do you want to be overflowing with grace? Then feed that fire. The more you nurture it, the greater your blessings will be. How can you ignite that fire? Start at Home by eliminating everything that destroys your spiritual hunger, including the distractions of material things.

I am not the first nor the only person to have faced tribulations and great challenges in life. I know your journey has not been easy either. I can imagine that, over coffee, you might share your stories with me. You have navigated turbulent valleys and faced many obstacles, but I also recognize the hard work you've put in to redirect your life. It hasn't been easy, and perhaps you haven't achieved the success you hoped for.

Remember that we all experience failures; sometimes, escaping difficult situations can feel impossible because they seem to catch up with you repeatedly. Please stay with me for a moment. I want to remind you that your past is just that—the past. Your current circumstances do not define your destiny.

There is something more waiting for you. That something is God. Deep in your heart, you know there is a power greater than the tribulations you're experiencing. You feel it, you perceive it, and you even dream of it. However, you may not know how to embrace this mercy that God has offered you. Even if it feels like you're only receiving a few crumbs, you need a voice to reassure you: "I am finally here."

Return to the house of God, where you find safety and protection—much like the feeling you get when you leave your Home and suddenly feel anxious to return, to relax, take off your shoes, get comfortable, and pour yourself a hot tea.

After facing so much trouble in the world, entering the house of the Lord brings a sense of rest, whether you are alone or with family. Sometimes, it's hard for our minds to understand why we are facing difficult circumstances. You may feel alone and lost. In such moments, talking to family, friends, or your pastor can be helpful. They often encourage you to ask God for help and to pray for guidance through your struggles.

At times, their words can feel simplistic and, at times, frustrating, especially when you don't feel immediate relief. It can feel suffocating, as if you lack the oxygen to breathe and keep going. But remember: God never abandons you. These struggles often signify that something great is on the horizon.

I want to remind you that when you experience spiritual hunger, don't expect to see blessings immediately filling that emptiness. The journey requires preparation for what is to come. If we wish to experience supernatural miracles, we must first pass through the tests that life presents. These challenges will come. We cannot move on to the next level without first conquering the one we are currently facing. I recall a tragic event that occurred in October 2017—something I had only seen in movies and never experienced firsthand. In the early morning of October 8, a series of fires known as "The Tubbs Fires" wreaked havoc, destroying more than 35,000 acres. Reflecting on that time, I still feel the strong emotions tied to that frightening event. The night before, as darkness fell, the air felt different.

## 13. LIVING WATER TO QUENCH SPIRITUAL THIRST

There was a strange wind that brought an unusual calmness, while simultaneously feeling mysterious and powerful. I remember sitting in the living room, trying to rest after a hectic day. Suddenly, the electricity went out, and I could hear the wind howling and branches hitting my window. At first, I didn't pay much attention to it. I decided to go to bed early. Using the light from my cell phone, I made my way to my room, changed into my pajamas, and threw myself under the covers, quickly falling into a deep sleep.

The sound of the wind lulled me, and I usually don't wake up during the night. I typically stay asleep until my alarm rings in the morning. However, that night was different. I woke up around 3:00 AM, feeling as though I needed to get up. I tried to turn on the lamp on my nightstand, but it wouldn't light up; the electricity was still out, and the wind outside grew louder. I grabbed my cell phone for light, but something in my Home felt wrong, as if I was caught in a bad dream, a precursor to something terrible.

A different feeling washed over me, prompting me to leave my bedroom and head to the hallway, then to the main door. When I opened the door, everything around me turned black. As I raised my eyes slightly, I was overwhelmed by a flood of red. In the background, I could hear the intense humming of the air, which carried flames from one side to the other. Witnessing that scene was chilling. At that moment, I was speechless; I couldn't scream or move—I was paralyzed, as if I remained motionless for hours. In front of me unfolded a horror movie: the sky was ablaze with bright red, and the relentless sound of the wind did not cease.

A dream came to my mind—one I had experienced several days earlier—where I sensed danger. Just like now, I looked at the sky and saw everything bathed in red. In that dream, I had to flee my house immediately, without the chance to grab anything. It was a premonition of what I was now facing.

That day, I saw the black smoke flooding the neighborhood and the glow of flames just a few meters away from me. I ran to wake my husband, insisting that we had to leave immediately. He was confused, struggling to understand my frantic screams as I rushed around the room, trying to change out of my pajamas. When he finally turned to look at the door, he saw the smoke already creeping into our Home. He quickly got dressed while I was almost outside. There was no time to grab our belongings; the flames were dangerously close to our house. I remember running from house to house, shouting for help.

Despite my fear, my first instinct was to warn our neighbors of the danger. These moments were intensely chaotic. Smoke filled my lungs, and it felt like I was sprinting at 100 miles per hour. Everything around me was dark; the only light came from the fire that had already consumed several nearby Homes. I could feel fireballs racing over my head, hear the distant screams of my neighbors, and the creaking of wood collapsing under the fire's heat. I was terrified—very scared. I covered my mouth with a wet t-shirt that I found and continued my frantic efforts to alert others about the fire. I could hardly breathe, and my heart was racing a thousand miles an hour.

We didn't have time to save anything from our Home, only our lives. My husband and I jumped into the car just before the flames reached us. It was a devastating day. I left behind a large part of my life in the flames—things that, despite being material possessions, held a very special meaning for me.

## 13. LIVING WATER TO QUENCH SPIRITUAL THIRST

Among them, I lost the letter my grandmother had written to me before she died. Although I never fully understood her handwriting, I felt I should have taken it out of the secret box where she kept it and given it to my mother so she could read it. My grandmother took the time to write something for me before she passed away, and it hurt my soul that I had never read her message.

That secret was consumed in the flames that morning. I also lost some napkins I had made as a child in Mexico, my native country, in a small town where I was born and raised until I was 13 years old. This was the place where I began to shape my path to who I am today. When relatives, acquaintances, and friends heard about the tragedy, they came to console me, saying, "Don't worry, you're fine, and that's what matters; you can recover everything you lost." But I knew I would never recover what I had lost, and I refused to listen to those comments.

Nothing made sense to me. I felt that no one understood what I was going through, and I would never recover from this—not because of the material things, but because of the traumatic experience that left deep scars on my heart. Many days of enormous bitterness passed like this, but then I came to understand that God never abandons us. If He had put me through this test, it was because He had something better in His plans for me. He always has a purpose, and perhaps that tragedy was meant to teach me a lesson. In the midst of spiritual hunger, tests often come that we must pass so He can use our pain as a platform for a greater calling.

If at any point you have felt defeated, abandoned, or have endured a tragedy or great loss, I understand you. Sometimes, you long to know the reason for everything that happens to you and get frustrated if you can't unravel life's mysteries. Now, if you're reading this, I want to assure you that you are still very much in time to start your journey back Home.

You can find your life's purpose at any moment. Just dig into your past, revisit your childhood, and reflect on your life little by little until you reach the present. I assure you that through this wonderful self-discovery, the truth will come to your mind like a flash; it will no longer be a secret. You will realize that experiences, events, tribulations, and even people will awaken you, help you rise, and encourage you not to give up. Maybe your path is more difficult because your calling is higher. Remember that problems will not destroy you; they will develop you and bless you.

Problems serve as the platform where our inner strength is cultivated. After this exploration, you will see that everything you have experienced has led you to your best version, something much greater than the problems and trials that currently afflict you. These experiences are merely preparation for the mission that God has in store for you.

We have previously discussed how many books and courses claim that by visualizing and manifesting, you can achieve your dreams. I must admit that I have read many of these books and spent a significant amount of money on courses that promised me the world, guiding my mindset solely by the ambition for material possessions.

After going through numerous disappointments, I realized that material things do not fulfill true dreams. Possessing our newest car, purchasing a house, or gathering luxuries, does not bring spiritual ful-

## 13. LIVING WATER TO QUENCH SPIRITUAL THIRST

fillment.In fact, it can lead to a never-ending desire for more, leaving one feeling increasingly empty.

It is essential to remember that how you nurture your spiritual life directly affects other areas of your life. Stop procrastinating your relationship with God; there are no more excuses. There is no guarantee for tomorrow. Now is the time to seek God. It is worth taking control of our lives with discipline and allowing Him to fill the void within us. Ultimately, the most crucial aspect of life is whether Jesus is our Lord and Savior.

As we have discussed in earlier chapters, go to Him, and He will come to you. Some people wonder why there are no more miracles like those described in the Bible. A friend I often speak with says he does not see God acting in his life, that miracles do not exist, and that God has abandoned us. However, this person is not approaching God and is not allowing Him to open his eyes.

There is no specific day to attend church or to pray; our relationship with God should be nurtured daily. Speak to God, and He will respond. Instead of asking, "Why doesn't God come to me? Why don't I see miraculous events in my life?", ask yourself, "Why don't I go to Him?" Jesus Christ wants you to be an empty vessel for Him to pour His blessings into you. You may wonder why you should be an "empty vessel." The answer is to empty ourselves of our ego, to stop believing that we know everything or can do everything on our own. We must empty ourselves to be filled with the Word of God, allowing Him to instill His wonders within us.

Throughout history, humanity has always sought the easiest path. Some have dedicated their lives to finding the "fountain of youth," a miraculous water believed to grant eternal life. Today, many still search for a magic source that will bring them success, satisfaction, and happiness. However, much of this searching is in vain. The true "living water" is the gospel of Jesus Christ, which can provide happiness, success, and eternal life to all people.

# 14

## The time is now

"Here I am, I stand at the door, and knock. If anyone hears My voice and opens the door, I will come in and dine with him, and he with Me," Revelation 3:20 (NKJV).

I understand that you have felt the weight of the world on your shoulders, and I want you to know how deeply sorry I am that you have had to go through such struggles. Although we may not have walked the same paths or faced the same challenges, I can relate to the pain that life can bring. However, I am convinced that there is someone incredibly loving and full of grace who has not abandoned you.

He is waiting patiently, wanting to comfort you and welcome you with open arms. I must tell you that if you are facing serious situations and trying to fight those battles with your own human strength, nothing will change. You will continue to find yourself in a vicious circle where one problem calms down, only to return again and again.

My life was like that for many years, and today I can say that until we take action, nothing will improve. You need to understand that the desert you are walking through has a purpose. "Awake, you who sleep, and be enlightened in Christ." God made us intelligent beings capable of choosing the narrow path. Even if it seems difficult to traverse, He grants us the wisdom and prudence to walk it well. If you don't know how to follow that path, ask God through prayer and by reading His Word. Avoid seeking advice from those who haven't been on that journey.

As a businesswoman, when I have doubts, I seek answers from successful individuals in the industry who have more experience than I do. I don't look for guidance from people who are just starting out. This principle is the same in your spiritual life. First, bow before His presence in prayer and engage with the scriptures: "Search the Scriptures; for you think that in them, you have eternal life" (John 5:39, NKJV). Then, seek out leaders who have traveled this narrow path for years to learn from them.

When I was at my lowest point, God lifted me from dry land and the paths where I walked alone, without faith and hope. Yet, He was always with me, patiently shepherding me until I could wake up and realize that I only had to rise from my deep sleep. Christ wanted to illuminate me with His wonderful light and lead me out of the desert to surrender at His feet. If God did that for me, He also wants to be present with you in that crucial moment of reconciliation; He wants to embrace you and restore your life.

Wake up! A new day is coming; it is knocking at your door, and it's time to cast aside all filth, every shadow of doubt and fear, and firmly grasp the purpose that God has for your life. It is time to stop being a spectator in your own life and to stop waiting for change to come on its own. Don't keep postponing your spiritual growth; don't

## 14. THE TIME IS NOW

look for excuses to avoid your commitment to God. Because it is a commitment we have—it's our duty.

We have a debt to Him. He has already paid the ultimate price with His blood for our eternal life. Now, it's our turn to become His disciples. Many say they do not feel the presence of God in their lives, but how could they when they are too busy with worldly distractions? If only they would set aside time to learn about what He has done for them and seek His presence!

I assure you, you will find Him and feel His presence. You will begin to see how He transforms your life, bringing clarity, strength, and a true relationship with your Creator. If everyone made an effort to purify their hearts and seek God sincerely, they would experience the transformation that the Holy Spirit brings to every aspect of their lives. Invite Christ to be the author of your story!

We desire to see God work great things in our lives and often feel that we are doing everything right. However, have we considered what He truly thinks about our actions?

We long for God to come to us, speak to us, and teach us His ways, yet we often remain stuck in disbelief. Many of us hesitate to move from our current mindset, where we continuously feed our egos with the notion, "That's how I grew up; these are my beliefs." We cling to this place of disbelief. Are you afraid of what others might say?

Do you fear stepping outside your comfort zone and feeling uncomfortable? Are you afraid of God and what He might ask of you? Are you fearful of the unknown and what the Lord might bring into your life? Or do you believe that the things of God are only for the overly zealous, choosing instead to enjoy life to the fullest because it is short, and you only live once? Which of these questions resonates with you the most?

Wouldn't you like for your life to be transformed? Perhaps you think to yourself, "I'm fine; I don't need to get closer to God. I follow His word from time to time, and that makes me feel good." The truth is, there is still much about Him that you don't know or understand. Once, someone said to me, "Why do you read so much scripture, attend so many church meetings, or participate in all those Bible studies? It's all so hectic.

We are going to die anyway, and it will take us…" Some of you can imagine the last word that person used. The truth is, it suggests the opposite of choosing eternal life with our Lord Jesus Christ. So now I ask: Why, if we have the words to affirm these beliefs, do we not use them to bless our lives instead of cursing ourselves?

We don't want anyone talking to us about the gospel or the glorious coming of Jesus Christ. When they do, we respond, "I know… I understand, I know…" But knowing and understanding alone do not save us. There is something much more important we must do after understanding: accept. By doing so, you will be ready for the next step—submerging yourself in the waters of baptism. You can ask your pastor or wherever you participate in Bible studies for more information on how to take this step toward eternal life. This path will offer you hope, as day by day, you prepare to live in the glory of God before

His presence, before the throne of His kingdom. "On a high and sublime throne…" There will be no more pain or tribulations, no more

## 14. THE TIME IS NOW

running around in anxiety or panic attacks, like the ones I endured and that countless people around the world experience. In that place, there will be eternal joy, and He will wipe away every tear. What beautiful words! They are not mine, but His promises to those who choose to accept Him and walk confidently by His side, knowing that one day they will see His beautiful face as it truly is. Now I understand that during all the time I spent away from His house, He never let me walk alone.

He was always with me, a guiding light to help me find my way back. He patiently shepherded this lost sheep, and at the moment He intended, He came to me with a greater purpose and rescued me in the blink of an eye. He left the 99 sheep to find me. It seems that during my time away from Him, when I stopped seeking His presence, it didn't trouble Him at all. I say this because, despite the distance and my disobedience, everything appeared to be going well in my life—it seemed wonderful from the world's perspective. I had a life of prosperity, success in business, and material wealth. You may also be feeling that you need nothing more, that you have everything—a perfect family, and no shortages in your life. But let me tell you, the shortage that the world is suffering from is immense, and it is often indescribable.

Many feel a deep need but are unable to express it. This situation has led great celebrities and wealthy businessmen to experience depression, contemplate suicide, or come to regret their missed opportunities for true fulfillment. I recall that the visionary in the field of computing and founder of Apple—the renowned technology company—wrote a letter from his hospital bed in the last days of his life. In that letter, he expressed something like this:

"I have reached the pinnacle of success in business. In the eyes of others, my life has been a symbol of success. However, apart from work, I have found little joy. Ultimately, my wealth has become nothing more than a familiar fact of my existence. Now, as I lie in this hospital bed and reflect on my life, I realize that all the praise and riches I once took pride in have become insignificant in the face of impending death.

In the darkness, looking at the green lights of the artificial respiration equipment and hearing the hum of its mechanical sounds, I feel the breath of death approaching. Only now do I understand that once we accumulate enough money for our lifetime, we must pursue other goals that are not related to wealth. How tragic it is to end our lives without that greater purpose. As the Bible says, "I press toward the goal for the prize of the upward call of God in Christ Jesus." (Philippians 3:14, NKJV).

I invite you not to let that great calling slip from your grasp for anything in the world, because the time may come when it is too late to reconsider, and you will not be able to rewrite your story in the book of life. In that moment, we risk losing everything. Why leave this to chance and take such a dangerous risk? God knows our days on earth, so it is wiser to respond to His call now rather than wait until the end of our lives."

I was always seeking to achieve more wealth from the material world to elevate my status, but His plans for me were different—perfect and better than my own. Despite the time I spent away, He knew what my destiny was. I hope this story provides you with a sign or advice that, regardless of your past or current situation, Almighty God is calling you amid your tribulations.

## 14. THE TIME IS NOW

He is waiting for you with open arms, requiring much more from you. He wants to listen to you, to know about you. He desires that you declare your love for Him, call upon Him, and serve Him. He seeks a total commitment from us to work within our lives. God wants you to be a warrior and live a victorious life. That is why He demands a closer relationship with you. He longs to spend time with you, to talk personally.

When you find yourself in front of Him, set aside all the distractions of this world—notifications, messages, calls, and social media alerts that only add to your confusion. Take time to be with Him. Ask Him what He wants from you and which paths you should take. In this anxious world, you need His guidance to make wise decisions. Heed His call, be thankful, and recognize the privilege of this opportunity. Do not assume that just because God is merciful, He will always be there.

At this moment, the Messiah is preparing for His second coming as the great conqueror that He is; His return will be glorious and majestic. How desolate it would be if, upon His return, He found us submerged in darkness, wandering lost in the desert, focusing on less important things. We find joy in the wrong pursuits, and He requires us to be alert and to announce the good news at all times. If you are still outside the house of the Lord, come back as soon as possible! He is waiting for you like a parent awaits their child; He cannot find peace until He sees you enter the doors of His Home. He has always been there, watching your steps like a lamp, reminding you that He is waiting for you.

I was lost in darkness for a long time, but a small light and a voice whispered to me: "Daughter, you walk through the world and cannot find a way out of this cycle of tragedies, problems, and frustrations. You are on the wrong path, but listen! Everything you are experiencing will soon come to an end. Believe in me."

Forget those false philosophies that only lead you to distance yourself from their promises, offering nothing but temporary gratifications. These material distractions steer our attention away from what truly matters—being by the side of the Lord and fulfilling the purpose He has for you. With the rise of social networks, a flood of information circulates, and many texts promise a life devoid of suffering—a supposedly perfect existence. They claim that by manifesting material things, you can achieve true happiness. They promise you wealth, jewelry, money, or even a successful marriage or business.

I share this from personal experience; I read those books, attended seminars, and even took online classes, but nothing made sense. It is all ultimately invalid. In fact, it only leads you down empty paths that can result in depression or even worse. I want to make it clear: everything I am sharing comes from my own life experiences. I have struggled with severe depression and feared for my life. I found no help from doctors, psychologists, or the countless books I read. Only Jesus Christ was able to alleviate my unbearable pain. In the past, I might have felt embarrassed to reveal my struggles; I envisioned writing a book focused on personal improvement and business. However, God had different plans for me.

Dear reader, you are not here by coincidence. Nothing happens by chance; everything is part of the perfect plan God has for each one of us, a plan not rooted in destruction, contrary to what the world offers. For a long time, I was lost, fulfilling society's expectations of me, which

## 14. THE TIME IS NOW

led me into deep depression. I felt worthless and reached a point where I was afraid of hurting myself. In that despair, I wondered, "Where are those people now who promised me the sky and the stars? Where is that philosophy of a wonderful life they preached?"

The truth is, nothing worked for me. The one who pulled me out of that dark hole was God. He spoke to me, saying, "Stop! Nothing you are doing is working and will never work, because I am the omnipotent God, the King of kings, and the Lord of lords." It was His words and love that lifted me from the mire. This is not a coincidence that you are reading this book.

God has brought us together so that through my story, you can reflect on where you come from, where you are going, and what comes next. You still have time. Share the gospel because the day will come when it will no longer be preached. The opportunity is now. No matter where you are in the world, you can take action and seek what the greatest teacher, the healer of healers, can do for your life and for your Home.

We live in a time of rapid technological advancement, but with these advancements come new challenges that can pose significant dangers to our well-being and spiritual lives. The image we present through our devices can differ greatly from our true lives, allowing negativity to undermine us daily and divert us from the purpose God has established for us.

We risk straying from our true essence and path. As children of God, we need the ability to make wise decisions regarding our resources and God's intentions for us. But how do we develop the spiritual capacity to act rightly?

Through prayer. We must cultivate a dedicated prayer life and seek the spirit of discernment to identify our daily priorities and tasks that deserve our attention, allowing us to fulfill our calling. If we neglect this aspect, we may become overwhelmed and struggle to carry the burdens we place on ourselves. How often have we heard of successful individuals who, despite their fame and wealth, took their own lives? We wonder why this happens when they seemingly have everything. The answer lies in what they lacked most: a relationship with Christ.

How do we foster a life with Christ? We do so through His Word, sincere prayer, and asking for His guidance to reveal the path He has laid out for us—a life filled with purpose. To be used by Him, we must do our part: remove negativity, bad habits, toxic relationships, and anything that distances us from God.

We need to let His light guide us, understanding that we cannot walk two paths simultaneously. We must choose between light and darkness. Living in darkness leaves us lost and unable to find truth and direction; we wander aimlessly, searching for answers in worldly people and situations, often forgetting that true truth is found in God's Word.

I recognize that you may be struggling to discover your true calling, and this is often due to not following the right path. Therefore, I urge you to make different choices; take the leap to cross the metaphorical river to the promised land, where you will find what God has prepared for you. Until you take that first step, God will not begin to guide you. Everything will transform once you decide to answer His call.

## 14. THE TIME IS NOW

Go to Him, and He will draw near to you. Once you make this decision, you will notice a significant change in your life—new directions and fresh horizons will open up for you. He will begin to communicate with you in ways you have never experienced, allowing Him to shape your life. I emphasize this because it is a mistake many have made in recent years: seeking purpose in shallow philosophies will never lead to genuine happiness.

It may become too late when you realize how far you have strayed from God and find yourself unsure of how to return to Him. "Seek the Lord while He may be found; call upon Him while He is near. Let the wicked forsake his way, and the unrighteous man his thoughts; and let him return to the Lord, for He will extend His mercy, and our God will generously offer His forgiveness. For My thoughts are not your thoughts, neither are your ways, My ways," says the Lord." – Isaiah 55:6-8 (NKJV).

Now, I want to remind you of the story of the Prodigal Son, which contains valuable lessons. I emphasize this narrative in this book because it is deeply moving, and I assure you that it can help you as much as it helped me during desperate moments when I sought peace in my life. This parable can be found in Luke 15:11-32 (NKJV). It tells the story of a father with two sons.

One day, the younger son asked his father for his share of the inheritance so that he could move far away and enjoy life. Although this request hurt the father deeply, he accepted his son's decision without arguing and gave him the inheritance. At first, the son was very happy. He left Home without a second thought, spending all his money on adventures, luxuries, and excesses. He believed he lacked nothing and thought he had found true happiness, forgetting the love and advice of his father.

Over time, the money ran out. The son squandered his last coins on vices and worldly pleasures, and that was when he realized his mistake. He found himself hungry, cold, and feeling utterly alone and repentant. Desperate, he tried to beg for money or food, but no one was willing to help him. Eventually, he even went to farmers to ask for the scraps they fed to their pigs.

The son recognized that he had fully enjoyed his inheritance, but it had ultimately brought him no real benefit. Feeling broke and desperate, he longed for more than just food—what he truly yearned for was to return to his father's house, where he had everything he needed.

In the same way, we sometimes distance ourselves from the presence of the Father. We think we can manage our lives better on our own, believing we don't need Him, but we are mistaken. Outside our Father's house, we lose everything. We lose our strength, our identity, and we become like beggars, facing a bankruptcy that is not merely financial; it concerns something far greater and more powerful—our very salvation, which God has prepared for those who choose to serve Him in His house.

Often, we flee from His presence, becoming unworthy of His love and mercy. However, realizing our mistakes and repenting, and then returning to His path, can lead to one of the most surprising and beautiful transformations a person can experience. Take, for example, the young man who decided to return to his father's house. He likely walked slowly, his head down, in dirty and torn clothes, feeling dis-

## 14. THE TIME IS NOW

appointed, ashamed, and fearful that his father would not welcome him or that he would be met with a barrage of questions or rejection. To his surprise, as he approached Home, his father saw him from a distance and ran to meet him, welcoming him with open arms.

The son then spoke, "Father, I have sinned against heaven and against you. I am no longer worthy to be called your son; make me like one of your hired servants." But the Father replied to His servants, "Bring out the best robe and put it on him; put a ring on his hand and sandals on his feet..." The longing and desperation the son felt to return Home overcame his fear of rejection. He didn't expect to be treated as a son again; he merely wanted to be back Home, under the command of the Father. When I say he got up, I don't mean in a superficial sense; I mean he experienced a resurrection, an awakening.

This son rose up, took the path marked for him once more, and left behind the wasteful life where he was lost and without hope. He approached his father, who restored hope to his life. Once back in the Home, he realized the care, protection, and comfort that existed there. He cried at the realization of everything he had lost by leading a worldly and meaningless life. The most beautiful aspect of this story is that the father did not go after his lost son; the son returned to his father's house.

That's why I emphasize that you only need to rise up and go to Him. Take action, and the Father will be waiting for you with open arms, lighting your way back. "Wake up, you who sleep, and Christ will shine on you." He will keep the light on so you can return Home from wherever you have wandered.

Just as the father of that young man ran to meet him when he saw him coming down the road, moved with compassion, so too will the heavenly Father run to us. The heavenly Father has a relationship of compassion with each of us that transcends our merits and deserving. The word "mercy" conveys the will to give everything of oneself, without limits. Just as God the Father gives us everything without reproach, as long as we come to meet Him, He will embrace us with infinite love when He sees us running toward Him.

All we need to do is decide to get up and return to Him, back to His house. We shouldn't worry about how to begin the journey; rather, we must draw strength from unexpected places to move forward. This parable of the prodigal son holds great meaning in my life. Unknowingly, I was that prodigal son who strayed from the Father for a long time but later returned, feeling defeated and unworthy yet carrying a kernel of faith that told me there was still hope and that my Father would offer me the best chance to start over.

This story has left a profound mark on me, and I know it has touched many others over the years. I never imagined that the thoughts I initially saw as fleeting would evolve into a testimony for you and for those seeking that "something" more.

I must confess that only God can fill the vast void that many people feel in this world. "For unto us a child is born, unto us a son is given, and the government will be upon his shoulder; and his name will be called Wonderful, Counselor, Mighty God, Everlasting Father, Prince of Peace." Isaiah 9:6 (NKJV), and His name is Jesus Christ. I wrote in a journal about the great need and emptiness I felt, and about the "reunion" I sought that would make me

## 14. THE TIME IS NOW

feel fulfilled, but my human perspective mistakenly related this to earthly successes.

God worked in my life in a profound way, and as I began to write this book, flashes of inspiration came to me. I realized that I am not the same person I was when I started; I have transformed into a different woman with new expectations and dreams. God spoke to me, gave me the title for this book, and entrusted me with the mission to share my journey of returning Home, much like the parable of the prodigal son.

I remember one day during the pandemic when my mother came to visit me. Those were difficult years when the government closed everything, and we were required to stay at Home with limited outings. Ironically, this situation was something God had already predestined in my life. I had to leave my business and other daily responsibilities behind to focus on writing this book. There was something unresolved between my mother and me. I often avoided being alone with her because I felt that she had something important to share, and I was afraid of that message—afraid to confront the truth.

However, one morning, I woke up early, made her a delicious breakfast, and we sat together for an hour over hot tea. She eventually picked up her Bible to read, while I grabbed a book, although I don't remember which one; at that time, most of my books were about prosperity, motivation, and personal growth. Suddenly, I heard my mother say, "Daughter, God is waiting for you with open arms to return Home.

Just like the prodigal son who left his father's house, God is waiting for you without reproach." In that moment, I felt as though

I had lost everything. I felt like a beggar in my own Home, and my inner self, screamed for help. I was refusing to confront the issues I had been carrying for years, going in circles while searching for a supposed truth. I longed to escape the desert I was in and yearned for living water.

Thanks to my mother and her words, guided by the word of God, I began to understand my path. She looked me in the eyes and said, "Daughter, the Lord is waiting for you. Do not turn your back on Him." Tears rolled down her cheek, and then she fell silent. At that moment, I had no response, and I didn't show any emotion; I felt frozen. But inside, I was crumbling. I remained in darkness until God began to illuminate my path. That moment pushed me closer to making the decision to return, as if all the questions I had sought elsewhere had just been resolved.

I was on the brink of changing the course of my life. If I was numb, it wasn't because I lacked feelings, but because they were overwhelming me. It felt like wounds within me were consuming me, and the decision I was about to make felt like a matter of life or death. A lump formed in my throat, making it hard to swallow, and I wanted to hide from everyone. I realized that my return Home was imminent and that something significant was on the horizon.

The reminder my mother provided while reading the Bible accelerated my process of returning to my Father. Just like the prodigal son who returned Home after losing everything, only to realize the abundance that awaited him, that is how I felt—helpless and hungry for God's word. I recognized that this hunger could not be satisfied by anything in the world. I had sought abundance in all the wrong

## 14. THE TIME IS NOW

places. I attempted to fill my hunger with shallow books and hollow philosophies that left me empty.

Though those books offered me an illusion of happiness, that joy dissipated quickly, and the hunger grew stronger. I even resorted to material possessions in an effort to fill the emptiness inside me. I was in survival mode when all I needed to do was raise the shield of faith to protect myself from the enemy's attacks and head toward the great reunion. Long before I even tried to answer His call, He was already waiting for me. He knew what I felt and was ready to satisfy my hunger with His word. There was no need for words; I felt His presence fill my entire being, and my heart overflowed with joy. A powerful shudder coursed through my body. With my return, there was a great celebration—a celebration of visions and wonders.

# Epilogue

I would have never imagined that my remedy for all my emptiness was to be back Home.

Many people asked me: "What happened to you? How did you achieve this transformation?" and my answer is always the same: "I came back Home. I came back to Him," because one day, I was blind and living in darkness, and now I can see and live in the light. That is the great secret; it was revealed to me.

God opened the doors of true success by revealing to me the purpose: to live in Christ Jesus, to grow day by day in the path of the Lord to reach our potential, to know and do the will of God for our lives, and to plant seeds that help others. To speak of His word and His promise so that souls can be saved and free from all bondage.

All my life, I have been looking to leave a legacy to my loved ones and a new generation. Now, through this book, through the words I leave written, I would like my life, the experience of my path, the pain, and my hope to be a message for you, dear reader, to know that God is always willing to help you take your life to other levels that you never imagined.

Today I want with this book to leave you a message on the road, to invite you to be attentive to feel the presence of God, to tell you that the riches of the material world are only temporary, because eternal happiness is at his side. And as the psalmist David says: "Make me know, Jehovah, my end, and when my days are almost over, show me how fragile I am."

Now, all I ask God is for him to help me remember for the rest of my life how short my time in this world is, that my days are numbered, and that I never stop praising Him or expressing my gratitude. These words I write are not meant to gain fame or boost my ego, but to bear witness to redemption. So that His name may be glorified all the time. When I was furthest from His presence, He remembered me and had mercy. He took me in His arms and illuminated my existence.

Some people do not believe in the prophetic prayers found in His word. Some say that every prophetic word has already passed, others say God is love, He cannot harm us, then they ask: "Why have such a strict life? Life is very short; we only live once." Assuming they are correct and that nothing of what was prophesied happens, everything will remain as it is, and nothing will be lost, but what if those people are wrong and every prophetic word is fulfilled? What would happen? You will have lost everything. Everything! And there will be no return.

As the Holy Scriptures say: "Lord, have we not prophesied in your name, and your name cast out demons, and in your name done many miracles? And he will answer, 'I never knew you; depart from me, you workers of iniquity.'" Matthew 7:22-23 (NKJV). Why should we risk everything for nothing? Why gamble with something that could cause us so much sadness? Through these pages, I invite you to join me in saying, if you'd like: Today, I find the light of God, and I long for eternal salvation, which is the most valuable thing I can possess. Today, I understand that every sacrifice has its reward, and there is no greater fulfillment than eternal life.

There is no time to delay; stop being lazy. Forget about saying, "I will do it tomorrow, next week, or next year." Right now, you may feel overwhelmed with a big project or a lot of work. I used to say all of those excuses as well, but you must be clear: there is no more time. There is nothing else to consider.

Something great is coming for you. Extend your hands to receive what lies ahead. Listen to the call of what is coming; you can already feel it. A powerful word is within you, challenging and expanding you. Soon, you will grow from within because you have faithfully believed, and you will receive your reward. Nothing will stop you from rising up and soaring to the place where God has destined you. You will see that God truly promised and fulfilled it.

"God is not a man that He should lie, nor a son of man that He should change His mind" (Numbers 23:19, NKJV). He is searching for people who not only aspire to make an impact in the world—an increasingly popular desire—but also for faithful individuals who will worship Him in spirit and truth. Will you be one of them? God is looking for courageous men and women who are willing to claim the blessings from heaven, and for that, obedience is essential.

I have come to realize that I no longer need to search for another path. Returning to darkness would be a tragedy for me. I have spent almost my entire life seeking the truth, looking for something that was already meant for me, yet I refused to accept it. Now I understand that God will not ask for my passport when I die, nor will He inquire about my bank account or personal documents. He will look at me with infinite mercy and be pleased with my actions, as long as I have walked with Him. He will say to me, "Well done, beloved servant!" That is why I shout to the world that we are living in the last days, and He is making His final calls. I know what it is to walk in darkness, and I am not willing to return to that place.

I am confident that I will find myself in the promised land, and I will never stop defending and helping others with my faith. In my daily prayers, I tell God that by His grace, I no longer need more reasons or convincing. Brothers and sisters who have accompanied me on this journey, believe me: you do not need any more reasons. Accept God into your heart; it is time to change your life and begin your return Home.

**"Return Home and tell how great things God has done for you." And he went away, telling throughout the city how great things Jesus had done for him." — Luke 8:39 (NKJV).**

INTRODUCTION

**f** Hilda Castaneda

**◉** @hildacastanedaofficial

**⊕** www.hildacastaneda.com

# ÍNDICE

Introduction . . . . . . . . . . . . . . . . . . . . . . . . . . . 13

1. Dreaming of a path to freedom . . . . . . . . . . . . . . 19
2. The path of rebellion . . . . . . . . . . . . . . . . . . . 31
3. A new pact for a transformative encounter . . . . . . . . 41
4. When earthly riches do not fill the heart . . . . . . . . . 55
5. Walking towards the light . . . . . . . . . . . . . . . . . 67
6. Paths through distant lands . . . . . . . . . . . . . . . . 83
7. The awakening of the heart . . . . . . . . . . . . . . . 103
8. The call . . . . . . . . . . . . . . . . . . . . . . . . . 115
9. Dying to live . . . . . . . . . . . . . . . . . . . . . . . 123
10. From being lost to being found . . . . . . . . . . . . . 135
11. Beyond reconciliation . . . . . . . . . . . . . . . . . . 153
12. Visions of the return: revelations along the way . . . . 163
13. Living water to quench spiritual thirst . . . . . . . . . 171
14. The time is now . . . . . . . . . . . . . . . . . . . . . 187

Epilogue . . . . . . . . . . . . . . . . . . . . . . . . . . . . 209

www.ingramcontent.com/pod-product-compliance
Lightning Source LLC
Chambersburg PA
CBHW032224080426
42735CB00008B/710